EXTRAORDINARY

# (EXTRA)ORDINARY

## (MORE)
## INSPIRATIONAL STORIES OF EVERYDAY PEOPLE

### KEITH MAGINN

Cover and book design by Mark Sullivan

ISBN 978-0-9985216-1-9 (paperback)
ISBN 978-0-9985216-2-6 (e-book)

Printed in the United States of America

Published by KiCam Projects
www.KiCamProjects.com

This book is dedicated to those who serve others
and try to make the world a better place,
that they have strength and wisdom;
and to all who are suffering,
that they may find relief.

# Contents

# Preface

With apologies to Mr. Dickens, the best of times and the worst of times might be right now. The world is a scary place today. We are a divided and frustrated human race, in many respects. Yet despite what you see in the news, there are still good people doing good things all over the world.

The late actor and activist Christopher Reeve said, "A hero is an ordinary individual who finds the strength to persevere and endure in spite of overwhelming odds." To me, the real heroes today aren't celebrities or athletes or politicians. They are "ordinary" people like the ones in this book. They are making a difference, often with little or no fanfare. And they give me hope.

*(Extra)Ordinary: More Inspirational Stories of Everyday People* is a collection of stories about ten amazing people. These tales aren't rainbows and unicorns from start to end, however. Many of these people went through extremely trying circumstances to get where they are now. But as Booker T. Washington said, "Success is to be measured not so much by the position that one has reached in life as by the obstacles which he has overcome."

I believe that people who have dealt with and overcome adversity are more relatable. Though some of the accounts depicted here are uncommon on the surface, each individual's struggles are universal and encouraging. The world needs more stories like these.

Being able to learn more about these people and to write about them has been an awesome and humbling experience. I learned from every one of them, and I am grateful they trusted me with their unique stories.

In many cases, these are people you would walk past on the street and never know they were what we might think of as "special." A few might stand out physically, but their stories go far deeper than simply what we see with our eyes.

Each of these people reminds us to see with our hearts and encourages us to ask questions, defy assumptions, and make real connections in a world increasingly characterized by virtual relationships. At a time when division runs rampant for various political, cultural, and social reasons, these stories can unite us all in the belief in the power of the individual to do more—and to be more—than we might initially believe or expect.

Faced with seemingly insurmountable problems, some people simply give up. Others do what they have to do to survive. Still others—a remarkable few—turn their experiences into a purpose to uplift others. As you will see, life's tests build depth and character. When we decide to keep fighting, we learn the human spirit is incredibly powerful.

The purpose of this book is to inspire you and also to challenge you, because it is becoming more and more apparent that we need more people like the ones you are about to meet.

What is your gift? What can you do to make the world a better place?

Thank you for reading.

All the best,
Keith Maginn
Winter 2017
Cincinnati, Ohio, USA

# John

January 17, 1987, was a typically hectic Saturday morning for the O'Leary family. Snow covered the ground on the cold winter day in St. Louis, Missouri. The family's matriarch, Susan, took daughters Laura and Cadey to the latter's singing lessons. Another O'Leary daughter, also named Susan, was getting dressed upstairs, while her sister Amy slept. The oldest O'Leary child, Jim, was asleep in the basement. The father, Denny, an attorney, was at his office, preparing to interview witnesses for an upcoming trial.

Before she'd left the house, Susan was alarmed to see that her nine-year-old son, John, had started a fire in the fireplace. She scolded him, saying he should never do that on his own again. She said she'd be back in an hour, then again reminded John to stay away from the fireplace.

She couldn't have known that moments later, her young son's curiosity would change the course of the future, propelling John on a journey from near death through extreme pain to becoming a world-recognized author and motivational speaker.

Earlier in the week, John had seen a few older boys from down the street produce a flash by tossing a match onto gas they'd sprinkled on the sidewalk. Fascinated, he decided to experiment with the same trick. With his parents away from home, John stuck a piece of rolled-up newspaper into the fireplace, lighting the paper, and took his "torch" with him to find the gas can in the garage.

Because the five-gallon can was too heavy for him, John put the burning newspaper on the ground and tilted the container to pour out a little gasoline. But invisible, highly flammable fumes escaped first, setting John's torch ablaze. The resulting explosion, heard blocks away, threw John twenty feet away into the wall on the far side of the garage.

Fire engulfed John. In a panic to get out of the garage, he darted back through the flames into the house, screaming for help. Sisters Susan and Amy came running down the steps, shrieking at the sight of their brother. Roused awake, Jim raced up the stairs from the basement. Without hesitating, Jim beat John with the doormat just inside the front door.

But Jim was unable to knock down the flames coming off his brother's body. Undeterred, Jim bravely went back into the fight, wrapping John in the mat, throwing him to the ground, and rolling on top of him. The flames died down but then reappeared. Jim told his sisters to call 911, then dragged John outside to the snow, which finally extinguished the fire.

John's two sisters rushed outside to help. Amy held her brother, trying to lessen his excruciating pain. She urged her brother to keep fighting, telling him everything would be okay.

Overcome by pain, John asked his older sister for a favor: "Go back in the house. I don't care if it's on fire. Go into the kitchen, get me a knife, come back out here, and kill me. Amy, just kill me!"

Amy told her brother to shut up and refused to let go. "Have faith and fight," she commanded.

Eight-year-old Susan heard this conversation. Determined to do her part, she ran back into the burning house, reappearing seconds later. Instead of bringing a knife, Susan threw a cup of water into John's face. She then made two more trips to refill the cup, each time tossing the water on her brother's face.

The firehouse was less than a mile from the O'Leary home, and emergency vehicles arrived two minutes after the call to take John three minutes away to St. John's Hospital. But severe damage already had occurred.

John's siblings called their dad's office to pass on the devastating news. Denny rushed to the hospital to be with John while mom Susan, contacted about an emergency at her house, raced home to find dark smoke pouring out of the second-story windows, which firemen were breaking in an attempt to extinguish the fire. Susan's children reported that John had been taken to the hospital after being badly burned.

When Susan arrived at the hospital, Denny told her John was not expected to live long, not even through the night.

John lay in intense pain in his bed in the burn unit on St. John's fourth floor. He knew his idyllic childhood—nice

house, devoted parents, fun vacations, love of sports—
would never be the same.

But his main concern was how his father would react to
the situation. *Oh my gosh, my dad is going to kill me!* John
thought. He had been in trouble for minor things before, but
now he had blown up the family's house.

When he heard his father enter his hospital room, young
John expected the worst. Instead, Denny said he had never
been more proud of John and told him he loved him. Those
words made all the difference in the world to a boy who
thought he had let everyone down.

When his mother arrived, John asked her if he was going
to die. Susan asked calmly if he wanted to die. John said no,
he wanted to live. Susan's response was direct, as is recalled
in the book she co-wrote with Denny, *Overwhelming Odds,*
in 2008:

> Then John, you are going to have to fight as hard as
> you ever have in your life…You are going to have
> to give it your all, and you won't be alone. Know
> that Daddy and I and Jesus will be with you each
> step of the way.
>
> John said, "I'll try, Mommy," before his parents
> were escorted from the room.

Susan and Denny took comfort in learning that St. John's and
chief surgeon Dr. Vatche Ayvazian were world-renowned
for burn care. The burn team wrapped John head to toe in
bandages, leaving only his eyes and nose uncovered. John

was intubated and given IV fluids. His extremities were strapped to the bed in an "X" shape to prevent him from moving. In just a few hours, his body swelled immensely.

A few hours later, Dr. Ayvazian—himself a survivor of serious burns as a child—leveled with John's parents. One hundred percent of John's body had been burned; eighty-seven percent was with worst-case third-degree burns. These were deep, penetrating all three levels of skin, through the muscle, and even to the bone in some areas.

The doctor said John had a one percent chance of living through the night.

John's mother collapsed into a chair upon hearing the prognosis.

Susan and Denny were warned that if their son did survive, his greatly weakened body would be susceptible to all types of dangerous conditions. Skin can regenerate in amazing ways, but not when burned to the third degree. The O'Learys were advised to take things one hour at a time.

Skin grafts from a small portion of John's scalp, his least-badly burned area, were his only chance at survival. *Overwhelming Odds* explains:

> The planned attempts at harvesting the same donor
> site six or more times to cover such a large area had
> not ever been done successfully. Survival from such
> significant injuries with insufficient donor sites was
> without precedent in the history of St. John's burn
> unit.

Defying the odds, John made it to Monday, January 19, and his first operation took place. Dead tissue needed to be surgically removed from John's body "in order to prepare a surface, which could successfully accept, nourish, and grow skin grafts," Susan writes in *Overwhelming Odds*. After an agonizing three-and-a-half-hour wait, Susan and Denny were told the procedure was a success. There was hope.

John had third-degree burns from his neck to his toes. But thanks to his sister's heroic efforts to throw water on her older brother, John didn't sustain third-degree burns on his face or scalp. The cooling of those areas protected what would become his donor site, essentially saving John's life.

Twice a day, nurses soaked John in a tub to loosen his bandages, then spent forty-five minutes removing them. They then dried, remedicated, and rewrapped John's body. The arduous dressing-change process took two hours each time, causing the young patient extreme pain.

Though it was risky, Dr. Ayvazian wanted John to start physical therapy as soon as possible to prevent his muscles from atrophying. He had twice-daily sessions, starting in his hospital bed for the first several months and moving to the first-floor therapy room for the last month or so.

"The pain was agonizing and progress seemed minimal," John's mother writes in her book.

John underwent numerous surgeries over the next few months, including thirteen skin graft operations. For weeks, he could communicate only by making a clicking sound when his parents pointed to the correct letter on an alphabet board. John had a few bouts of pneumonia, as well as a life-threatening bacterial infection, while fighting to recover. His condition was considered critical for his entire stay at St. John's.

Thankfully, a few people showed up in John's life to make things more bearable.

The day after arriving in the unit, John got an unexpected visitor. A huge St. Louis Cardinals baseball fan, John listened to as many games on the radio as possible. He knew the sound of the legendary "voice of the Cardinals," Jack Buck, well. Hearing his voice in person while strapped to his hospital bed surprised John.

Buck told John to keep fighting. He promised the Cardinals would host a special day for him when John got out of the hospital. Buck then left John's room, shut the door, and collapsed into tears.

He spoke with a nurse, who said there was no chance John would survive. Still, Buck returned the next day to encourage his new friend. For months, Buck dropped in to the burn unit frequently, and during broadcasts, Buck often mentioned his "little friend, John O'Leary." He encouraged several Cardinals players to visit the hospital as well.

The Saturday after the accident, another selfless man came to meet John. St. Louis Blues hockey player Gino Cavallini assured John that the entire Blues team was pulling for him. Cavallini even made a bold promise: Not only would St. Louis win that night—against the same team that had beaten the Blues the previous night—but he would score a goal for John.

Because Cavallini was better known for fighting than for scoring goals, John had his doubts. But he and his parents tuned in to the radio nonetheless. True to his word, with only a few minutes remaining in a tied game, Cavallini put a shot into the net, securing the win for his team. Cavallini and many of his teammates cried tears of joy, and Cavallini was named player of the game.

Despite his own predicament, John was overjoyed. After he finally managed to fall asleep, a commotion in the hallway outside his room awakened him. Cavallini and many of his teammates had come to the burn unit with soda and a few dozen pizzas to celebrate with the brave patient. They presented John with the hockey stick Cavallini used to score the goal, which had been autographed by the entire team, and Cavallini's jersey. John's new friends stayed until almost two in the morning.

Cavallini returned several more times in the following weeks, sharing that everywhere he went, people asked him how John was doing. When Susan and Denny thanked Cavallini for his incredible compassion, Cavallini replied: "Don't thank me. It has been my privilege to spend time with John. He has taught me about courage, strength, and perseverance, beyond my imagination."

In February, another special guest was permitted to visit. This was not a professional athlete or celebrity, but John's hero—his older brother, Jim, who had sustained first-degree burns on his hands and arms when he rescued John. John had been anxiously awaiting this opportunity, and he expressed his deep gratitude by clicking out that Jim had saved his life. Both brothers broke into tears.

Beyond the occasional bright spots, serious obstacles remained for John. Due to the severe damage, all of his fingers and both thumbs had to be amputated. John was left with only small portions of some of his fingers. Signing the consent form to approve the amputations was the most difficult thing Denny had ever had to do, and John was devastated.

John was released from the hospital after one hundred thirty-two days—nearly five months—on May 29, 1987. His two daily physical therapy sessions would continue at St. John's, as would a medical review at the burn clinic every Saturday morning, but John was going home. Denny showed his appreciation to the amazing staff by rolling in a wheelbarrow loaded with bottles of Champagne and Life Savers candy.

His son was wheeled out of the burn unit amongst cheers and tears. The entire team that had cared for John was on hand to wish him well. When he arrived home, a throng of John's classmates, teachers, neighbors, family, and friends welcomed him with balloons and banners.

A month and a half after John's release, John and his family joined Jack Buck for "John O'Leary Day" at Busch Stadium on July 10, 1987. Buck gave John a tour of the Cardinals' clubhouse and locker room, where he introduced the young super-fan to the players. John asked big-hitter Jack Clark to hit a home run.

John sat in the announcing booth with Buck, while the latter called the game and interviewed John on air. The hometown fans were treated to an exciting battle won by a Clark single—perhaps not as dramatic as a home run, but a game-winning hit in extra innings is almost as good!

John drank eight Cokes during the game. Buck noticed that John used a straw while his mother held the cups for him. That's when Buck decided to make even more of a difference in John's recovery.

A few days after the game, John received a baseball autographed by Cardinals superstar shortstop Ozzie Smith. A note from Buck accompanied the ball, saying if John wanted a signed ball from another player, all he had to do was write a thank-you note to Smith.

Due to the amputations of his fingers, John was able to write only an "X" until then, but this new challenge got his attention. After all, he wanted more autographs! With much effort, John wrote sixty notes and got sixty autographed balls by the time his Cardinals played in the World Series that October.

Buck was inducted into the Baseball Hall of Fame that summer, and in his acceptance speech, he mentioned John O'Leary: "as gutsy a person as I had ever met."

In order to get out of his wheelchair, John continued grueling physical therapy at St. John's for several months. John would sometimes cry on the way to the hospital because the sessions were so intense, but he still went. His nurses conducted the most painful treatment in a broom closet with a rag in John's mouth to stifle his screams.

It was nine months before John could stand up. One of his favorite therapists was Nurse Roy, who looked like the character Apollo Creed played by Carl Weathers in the *Rocky* movies. Before John believed it was possible for himself, Roy was in his ear. "Boy, you are going to walk again," he'd tell John. "You might as well get used to it. I'll walk with you." Slowly, John learned to walk again, learned to ride a bike, and learned to run, though awkwardly.

John's mummy wrap of bandages came off after eight months. But, self-conscious about his scars, John kept his body covered as much as possible. He hid his scars, first under the Jobst body suit he had to wear for about a year, and then under the pants and long sleeves he chose to wear year-round.

"I remained bound with self-imposed bandages," John says. "Not just for that first summer but for the two decades that followed."

Meanwhile, the kindness of the O'Learys' community continued. John received more than a thousand cards and letters during his recovery, including from President Ronald Reagan and Pope John Paul II. A family friend organized volunteers to bring meals to the family five nights a week for eight months. Another friend ran a blood drive in case John needed donors. One hundred individuals gave a unit of blood each, including older brother Jim's entire DeSmet High School junior class.

Still other friends took on the task of cleaning up the fire damage to the O'Leary home and their belongings, inventorying every item for insurance purposes. While Susan and Denny's home was refurbished, a couple they barely knew from church generously offered their five-bedroom home while they vacationed in Florida for several weeks. Two nurse friends took turns taking care of John's dressing changes every other day for months, and a group of mothers rotated driving John to his physical therapy appointments at the hospital, again for months.

Meanwhile, John's medical bills cost more than $4,000 a day. Susan and Denny's insurance limit would not be nearly enough to cover everything. "Incredibly, the amount of the group insurance was raised for the entire national group from the $250,000 limit to $1,000,000 midway through John's hospitalization," Susan writes in *Overwhelming Odds*. "This falls, also, in the category of miraculous."

In March 1988, another man stepped forward to support John. Seventy-eight-year-old motivational speaker Glenn Cunningham drove his pick-up truck to St. Louis from his farm in Arkansas to meet the young survivor. Cunningham had won the silver medal in the 1,500-meter run in the 1936 Olympics in Munich, Germany.

What made Cunningham's Olympic feat truly astounding was that he'd been badly burned at age seven in an explosion that killed his older brother and best friend. Doctors almost amputated Cunningham's legs but gave in to his mother's pleas to save them. After years of struggle, Cunningham went on to become one of the fastest runners in the world.

While they walked together, Cunningham told John: "I didn't think I'd end up at the Olympics. All I knew was I wasn't going to live my life sitting down. So I got up. I put one foot in front of the other. And I never looked back and never quit."

Cunningham's greatest contributions to mankind came from his heart for helping troubled youths, many without loving homes, who moved onto the farm with Cunningham, his wife, and their twelve biological children. The Cunninghams' forty-year ministry served more than a thousand individuals, often eighty to ninety at a time.

Cunningham heard about John's story and showed up fourteen months after the accident. He shared his story and inspired John to set goals for himself, to pursue his dreams with passion. Everything John desired would be possible, Cunningham assured him, just when the young-ster was disheartened about what his future looked like. Cunningham advised John, above all, to never give up.

John would turn out to be Cunningham's last pupil. Cunningham returned home to his farm and died two weeks later.

Newly inspired, John worked with a tutor and caught up on all the schoolwork he had missed, rejoining his class that fall. He later got a non-restricted driver's license and graduated from DeSmet High School in 1995. John then moved onto the campus of St. Louis University (SLU), where he got a finance degree in 1999.

The friendship between John and Jack Buck continued. The Cardinals' radio announcer made a standing offer that John could visit the broadcast booth any time he attended a baseball game, which John did often in his high school and college years. For John's college graduation, Buck gave him a special gift: the crystal baseball that Buck had been given at his Hall of Fame induction in 1987, the same year John was burned.

Buck died from complications of Parkinson's disease at the age of seventy-seven in the summer of 2002. John remains eternally grateful to this remarkable man, a generous and empathetic soul who taught him that a simple act of kindness can change the world.

In honor of Buck—as well as Denny, diagnosed with Parkinson's in 1993—John started a fundraiser. His three events raised more than $35,000 for the Michael J. Fox Parkinson's Foundation. Joe Buck, Jack Buck's son and a well-respected sports announcer in his own right, said, "If my dad were sitting here today, he would tell you he is more proud of John than anybody else he met in his life."

John worried for years that he'd never have a serious girlfriend. His humor and magnetic personality attracted a lot of friends, many female, but he went through high school and college without dating. John wondered if he would find someone to love, and someone who loved him.

During his junior year at SLU, John met Beth Hittler, a freshman, at a fraternity dance. They became good friends over the next year, but John's feelings grew stronger. He finally got up the nerve to ask her to be his girlfriend; Beth responded that she thought of John more like a brother.

Though crushed, John persisted. Another year passed and he tried again but was met with the same reply. Their friendship continued, and eventually Beth's feelings for John grew into love.

Three years later, in 2003, Beth and John got married. More than four hundred guests were invited to the wedding. At the reception, John thanked the doctors, nurses, his family, and his brother, Jim, for saving his life. (The entire medical team that had assisted John was in attendance, except for Nurse Roy, who couldn't be located.) John then turned to his bride, proclaiming himself the luckiest man in the world.

"November 22, 2003, was without question the happiest day of my life…marking the culmination of a miraculous journey," John's mother writes in *Overwhelming Odds*.

Until that day, the O'Learys didn't talk much about the accident. But seeing John's story unfold so beautifully on his wedding day, Susan and Denny were inspired to share the story of the fire—a tragedy transformed into a tale of hope and inspiration. Initially, John didn't understand their desire to write the book, but they were confident they had a story that needed to be told, and John eventually supported their project.

Susan and Denny printed just two hundred copies of their book to share with friends and family, a thank you for helping them overcome the fire. The book ended up changing the course of John's life.

John had kept his story as quiet as possible throughout high school and college, but now it was out for the world to see, and he could no longer hide. After his early reluctance, John read the book—what John lovingly refers to as his "unauthorized biography"—and realized his difficult situation was actually a gift.

John finally embraced the events of his life, tearing down walls he'd created to protect himself for twenty years. He had a new purpose: to own his story and to celebrate his scars. After all, John reasoned, exposing our true selves to others enables us to live honestly and to connect with and inspire others.

"By denying what happened to me," he says, "I denied the world the chance to hear about the miracle of my survival, the wonder of my life, and the magnificent potential of theirs."

John was in his seventh year as a real estate developer when he got a call. The woman on the other end had read his parents' book and wanted *him* to share his story with the group she led. Tempted to say no, John instead said yes.

John had never told anyone his full story, not even his

closest friends. Not even Beth. But he'd now accepted an invitation, a challenge really, to speak to a group for fifteen minutes about all he'd been through.

Public speaking terrified John, but he was intent on making good on his pledge, so he practiced for more than forty hours. He pulled up to the event location, threw up, and ignored the negative voice in his head telling him to just go home.

John walked into the classroom and managed to get through his first speech. When he finished, the four third-grade Girl Scouts gave him a round of applause and a hug.

Though this wasn't exactly instant stardom, it was a defining moment in John's life. "I've learned again and again in life that you can show courage or you can be comfortable," he says. "But you can't do both at the same time. While comfort might be popular, courage changes lives."

Gradually, John repeated his story more and more. Interest grew, as did his confidence. Instead of merely accepting offers, he began seeking opportunities to speak. A speaking business evolved and he got out of real estate in 2007 to focus solely on his new venture. At twenty-eight years old, he founded his company, Rising Above.

John had found his purpose, and from there, things took off.

When he looked at the picture of himself as a boy on the cover of his parents' book, John saw something new. "I no longer saw a little boy at the end of a journey he had barely survived," John says, "but instead at the start of one that he could not wait to begin."

Two years after their wedding, Beth and John had a baby boy. They named him Jack.

Beth and John have been happily married for almost fourteen years. They are active in their church and have four healthy kids: three boys and a girl, ages five to eleven. John is extremely grateful for his family: "They were absolutely worth the wait. True love always is worth the wait."

After originally printing two hundred copies of *Overwhelming Odds* for family and friends, Susan and Denny O'Leary have now sold more than sixty thousand books. The introduction sums up the book beautifully: "This is the true story of a boy, his family, a community, and a God who persevered against overwhelming odds."

"January 17, 1987 is a date forever embedded in our hearts," Susan and Denny write. "It is the day that our family embarked on a journey that forced us to come face to face with tragedy, ourselves, and our God in a way never before even contemplated."

A long way from that first Girl Scouts speech, John has released a DVD, *The Power of One*, a presentation in front of a crowd of eight thousand in St. Louis in 2015. After all John had endured, he stood in front of others, inspiring them to make an impact on the world in their own way. He challenged those in attendance to focus on the possibility of the future, on the positives in life instead of the negatives.

During the talk, John shared a story from 2011, when he

had given a series of presentations to the Alabama Power Company. As a thank you for his help, they'd given John a surprise. The company had paid a private investigator to track down Nurse Roy. During their emotional reunion, Roy expressed astonishment in realizing after twenty-seven years that his own life and the work he did as a nurse had mattered.

John invited the people in the St. Louis crowd to ask themselves, whether in their home life, faith life, or work life, "What more can I do?" Because of John's sense of humor, many laughed throughout his speech; because of what he went through, many cried. At the end, everyone stood and cheered.

John published the national bestselling book *On Fire: The 7 Choices to Ignite a Radically Inspired Life* at the beginning of 2016. His book, dedicated to Beth, tells his remarkable story and outlines seven choices that helped John survive and thrive.

Despite indescribable pain, five months in the hospital, multiple surgeries, amputations, and years of physical therapy to regain mobility, John says in his book that if he had to do it all over again, he wouldn't change a thing:

> So, while it is true that if I'd not been burned, I'd remove all the difficulties caused by the fire, it is also true that I'd destroy all the gifts galvanized because of it.
>
> You see, everything beautiful and enriching in my life today was born through the tragedy of those

flames. Through the painful ashes of recovery as a child, I grew in character, audacity, compassion, faithfulness, and drive. It led to a clear perspective on what actually matters and a bold vision for what's possible. Because of the fire, I don't take things for granted, am grateful for each day, and am certain that the best is yet to come…

…Today I live an awesome life; a radically inspired life.

John's Rising Above organization is dedicated to inspiring others. He speaks to fifty thousand people annually, hosts his own "Live Inspired" podcast, blogs, and contributes to publications like *Parade Magazine* and The Huffington Post. John has shared his message with more than 1,200 organizations and churches around the world, including Southwest Airlines, LEGO, PepsiCo, and Enterprise Rent-A-Car.

Doctors gave nine-year-old John O'Leary only a one percent chance to live. It turns out, that was all the chance John needed.

"You can't always choose the path that you walk in life," John says, "but you can always choose the manner in which you walk it."

You can learn more about John O'Leary at JohnOLearyInspires. com. If you would like to make a donation in honor of John O'Leary, please do so to the Phoenix Society for Burn Survivors, a nonprofit for which John is a board member.

# Anna

Anna Renault could have died many times by now. In fact, she often wonders how she is still alive. Somehow, she has prevailed, and she now uses her love of writing to spread the word about how others can be not only survivors, but thrivers.

Anna was born and raised in east Baltimore, Maryland. She was born with a heart murmur, a serious and sometimes fatal condition at that time. To minimize threats to her health, doctors prescribed a sedentary lifestyle. But years later, doctors realized exercise actually would strengthen her heart, so Anna became quite active.

She became a baton twirler, taking part in numerous parades. Her heart grew stronger and ceased to be a concern, but Anna was plagued by various mishaps throughout her childhood and teenage years.

"I was a frequent flyer at the local emergency room at Baltimore City Hospital," she writes in her book *Anna's Journey: My 40 Year Dance with Cancer*. "There were days when I wondered if I was cursed…if I was a magnet that attracted trouble."

At fourteen, Anna had her first near-death experience, recounted in her first book, *Anna's Journey: How Many Lives*

*Does One Person Get?* A sudden storm produced lightning that struck a tree, killing two people standing near her. The area all around her was electrically charged; to this day, Anna wonders how she walked away unscathed.

Just seventeen months later, another tragedy shook her world. Anna's boyfriend, Gene, had been drafted into the U.S. Army for the Vietnam War, and he proposed on December 9, 1965, just before he was to leave for boot camp. The couple planned to elope but never got the chance. Due to a faulty latch, Gene's car door flew open that night, and in his desperation to close it, Gene swerved off the road into the woods. Anna was not hurt, but Gene was killed when the open car door hit a telephone pole before the vehicle slammed into a tree.

As best she could, Anna moved on. She returned to her Catholic school but quit for ten months before resuming her education in a public school. She ended up marrying her crush—the local bad boy—and graduated high school in 1969 at age nineteen, pregnant with a baby girl she would deliver on New Year's Eve.

During her marriage, Anna was the victim of domestic violence at the hands of her alcohol- and drug-addicted husband. His abuse sent her to the emergency room more than once. Her marriage broke up in 1974 when Anna was twenty-five years old.

Anna credits her belief in God for getting her through the abusive relationship. When it ended, she felt strong and happy. Life was good.

She joined a single-parent organization, "Parents Without Partners," which got Anna and her five-year-old involved in fun activities with many new friends. They stayed busy, enjoying bowling, camping trips, picnicking, hiking, and skating. "My daughter and I enjoyed a life free from the fear with which we had lived during the rough times of the violence related to drunkenness and then drug abuse," Anna says.

Despite her happiness, Anna felt a little "off," which she attributed to being too busy. She went for a physical in April 1976 and was told to see if slowing down helped. Anna got the sense the doctor didn't take her concerns seriously.

She went to her gynecologist that May (because her grand-mother died from uterine cancer, Anna kept these regular appointments) and again was advised to slow down. Some tests were done, but all came back normal. But Anna knew something wasn't right.

Heeding her doctors' advice, Anna laid low in the fall of 1976. She took her daughter bowling and to the skating rink but watched the fun from the sidelines. Despite her reduced activity level, Anna was losing weight, had no energy, and still was not improving. Her menstrual cycle and bowels acted strangely, but she feared a trip to the doctor would result in another lecture. In her book, she explains:

> In 1976, my body was screaming loud and clear
> that something was wrong. I made attempts to treat
> this symptom, then that one, but treatments either

didn't work, or doctors were reluctant to provide any. More than one doctor strongly suggested that my problems could be resolved with psychiatric treatment…the problems were all in my head!

The single mother avoided medical intervention until her annual checkup in 1977. Her doctor ran some tests, but Anna looked young and healthy, which seemed to play a part in her lack of a diagnosis.

Anna recalls:

Even when the first doctor had positive test results, he told me I was too young to even consider having cancer, especially uterine. It seemed to be more acceptable to tell a young woman, who looked healthy, that she was depressed…that she was having a delayed reaction to her domestic violence, separation and divorce, and that she was overdoing it with activities she wasn't in the habit of doing and was simply out of shape.

Because the doctor did not believe the findings, more tests were run. They came back positive again. A third round of tests was ordered, but the findings were the same: At twenty-seven, with a seven-year-old daughter, Anna was diagnosed with uterine cancer.

After the multiple tests and the weeks of worry, Anna changed doctors. She found a competent and compassionate doctor and underwent a life-saving surgery to eradicate the cancer. Despite some complications that kept her away from work for fourteen weeks instead of the planned six, she was given a clean bill of health. Anna thanked God often and prayed she'd live long enough to see her daughter graduate high school and perhaps become a mother herself someday.

In 1982, Anna had surgery to remove melanoma on her chin. Then two years later, she had another procedure for squamous cell carcinoma on her back. Other than these skin cancers, her health was good.

Anna's close calls with death continued, however. Upon returning home from an appointment in 1988, Anna and her pregnant daughter heard the smoke detectors going off. She writes in *Anna's Journey: How Many Lives Does One Person Get?*: "We opened the front door, which apparently added oxygen to the not-yet-flashed-over fire outbreak. When we opened that front door, flash-over did occur and blew out the back of the house."

Once again, Anna was untouched in the explosion, which burned the house to the ground. Her granddaughter was born two weeks later.

In 1988, after fainting at Disney World, Anna learned she had connective tissue disease requiring treatment for lupus. She was put on a treatment plan to control her aches and address inflammation of her lungs and kidneys.

In 1994, Anna's health woes continued. She started having bowel changes and abdominal pain. Her toenails and the hair on her legs stopped growing. Anna knew something was seriously wrong:

I went to a gastroenterologist demanding the colonoscopy that would save my life. It is also unfortunate that the health insurance system tends to run our health care. I was told I was not eligible for the test because I was too young. At forty-four, people were not supposed to get colon cancer! I was told the insurance would not cover the test until I was fifty.

Knowing my personal history with cancer, and knowing my family history with the disease, I fought the insurance system.

After numerous failed attempts, Anna finally found someone who approved the crucial tests. Sure enough, the results indicated cancer in the descending colon. She underwent another surgery—her fourth to remove cancer—and this time the doctor prescribed chemotherapy, which Anna agreed to, eager to guarantee the cancer was gone for good.

Despite her circumstances, Anna says she never considered giving up. Medicine had come a long way and advancements were happening all the time, so why quit? With hope and prayer, she'd won every battle to that point, so she'd continue fighting until medical research came up with an answer.

She focused on learning as much as she could about her medical condition and about the top specialist in that field. "I should go to medical school," she says, laughing. "With all my experience, I feel like I could pass all the tests."

Chemotherapy was hard on Anna, making her seriously ill. She stopped the treatment, reassured by the doctor's claim that all the cancer was removed and chemo was simply a preventative measure. Anna's comfort didn't last long.

In the fall of 1996, Anna noticed the tell-tale signs that her cancer was back. A colonoscopy confirmed her suspicions. At forty-six years old, she had cancer in her ascending colon. Anna refused chemo after another surgery.

In 2005, an unrelated CT scan of Anna's abdomen for a stomach bleed led to a complete surprise. The test showed ovarian tumors, so Anna went under the knife yet again. In March, she was set for the removal of the tumors and her ovaries, but complications during surgery left the ovaries intact. In the recovery room, the doctor told Anna she had almost died on the operating table due to serious bleeding.

"I never asked, 'Why me?'" Anna says. "I believe in God, and I believe God gives you what you can handle. Cancer is in my family. How do you counteract genetics? Asking that doesn't solve anything or make me feel better. It doesn't do anything to help. It's a waste of time."

By August, significant abdominal pain let Anna know the ovarian cancer was back; by September, her toenails and leg hair had stopped growing again. She recalls:

> When I suspected my first colon cancer (1994), I noticed these strange symptoms. My doctors thought, once again, that I must be nuts. They didn't want to hear that someone under fifty even

suspected colon cancer. The doctor I saw argued that it wasn't cancer if I had symptoms, because colon cancer reportedly doesn't have symptoms. He was the one who quickly recommended that I go to a psychiatrist for treatment. He felt I was cancer-crazy because I had other types of cancer.

Further testing confirmed Anna's suspicions, detecting three more tumors. Perhaps spooked by her last procedure, she was more fearful and cautious for this surgery, as she writes in *Anna's Journey: How Many Lives Does One Person Get?*:

To be honest, I was seriously scared that I would not survive the surgery in September 2005. I was so concerned that I made contact with a local funeral parlor and pre-paid my funeral expenses, completed the information for the obituary column, and updated my will. A living will was also prepared—just in case.

Despite her trepidation, the surgery was successful. Anna was cancer-free. She remains grateful to her "angels," dear friends who supported her emotionally during those rough times. These caring souls reached out to help with grocery shopping, laundry, and many other chores. And Anna would lean on her support network again soon.

In 2008, Anna was getting tired too quickly and had to buy a smaller belt from losing so much weight. Blood work in November said everything was fine, but Anna, then fifty-nine, knew better. Feeling unheard once again, she switched doctors, relieved to finally have a team of doctors willing to listen. A mammogram and MRI in May 2009 found breast cancer, requiring two surgeries, along with chemo followed by radiation.

Anna's breast cancer chemo lasted four months, leaving her bald for nine months. In February, as the Blizzard of 2010 ("the storm of the century") dumped twenty-five inches of snow on Baltimore, Anna started thirty-six treatments of radiation therapy, held five days a week. With the chemo, radiation, and unpleasant side effects—some nausea, a lot of diarrhea, and dehydration six different times—she was at the end of her rope and prayed for strength to get through.

Again, her network of angels swooped in. Friends and anonymous donors sent Anna food baskets, medical and household supplies, and grocery store gift cards; ran a fundraiser in her honor to offset mounting bills; and more. Their generosity was a godsend.

Anna had retired from Maryland's Department of Education's Division of Rehabilitation Services in April 2001 after more than thirty-one years. At the time, doctors thought Anna might have a brain tumor. Financially stable and not knowing how much longer she'd have to live, she chose to walk away from her career.

"I retired at fifty-one, which was the best thing I ever did for myself," she explains. "The stress of my job alone would have made my health even worse."

Fortunately, Anna did not have a brain tumor, but the father of her daughter's two oldest children suddenly moved out, leaving Anna the main breadwinner of the family. In 2010, she was living off a small pension and low-paying part-time jobs. Anna says she wouldn't have survived those lean times without her friends' charitable assistance.

The selfless support of friends also helped ward off depression, a common result of cancer, chemo, and radiation treatment. Anna says:

> The breast cancer was the toughest journey at that point in my life. I did promise the doctor that I would accept whatever chemo he prescribed and that I would finish it to the end regardless of the tough side effects. I truly believed it was in my best interest to tough it out...to do whatever was necessary to ensure that cancer was gone—gone for good...at least I hoped and prayed it was the right decision. I had no idea just how tough the journey would be...but I kept my promise!

When the Affordable Care Act took effect in 2010, the American Cancer Society sent a request looking for volunteers willing to share what the new health care statute meant to them. Anna agreed and was surprised to be contacted for a phone interview. She was even more shocked when ABC News asked her to appear along with the Secretary of Health and Human Services for an on-camera interview in Washington, D.C.

"I felt like a criminal going through all of the security, and I was thinking, '*You* invited *me* here,'" she says, chuckling. "I thought, 'What have I gotten myself into now?'"

But Anna was passionate about the topic. Though her knees knocked nervously, Anna was pleased with how she handled being on a national news show. She was glad to be given the opportunity to highlight the good aspects of the act from her perspective.

Back in Baltimore, her treatment lasted nearly two years in all. Thrilled to be alive, Anna was grateful for the excellent care she received. Hearing "no evidence of disease" was her goal each time she fought cancer, she says:

> We all want to hear the pronouncement, "The cancer is gone!" We all pray for the day that treatment is finished and that we can get back to the business of living what is often considered a normal life…no running to and from the doctor for treatments, dealing with side effects and unusual aches and pains.

But Anna's fight was *still* not over. After noticing some odd symptoms in December 2014, she went in for blood testing. One evening in March 2015, her oncologist called to say they needed to move quickly—Anna's blood cell count numbers had tripled. Several scans confirmed metastatic breast cancer.

Anna, then sixty-five, endured her ninth bout with cancer.

Now at sixty-seven, Anna is still in treatment for metastatic breast cancer. She says, "I'm old!" but then adds, "People didn't think I'd see fifty...or sixty...so I will take it." She hopes a breakthrough cure for cancer will happen in her lifetime and counts her blessings that she lives in Baltimore, home to some of the top specialists and best medical facilities in the world.

Anna says she thanked God for guiding her to a job that provided her with health insurance and paid sick leave. She could focus on getting better; however, some patients are not so fortunate, as Anna writes in *Anna's Journey: My 40 Year Dance with Cancer*:

> Bankruptcy due to medical bills is a real fact of life. Becoming homeless and destitute due to a long battle with cancer is also a true fact of life for many. It is a real problem that needs serious consideration and a permanent fix by our government—on the federal level, as well as state and local levels. Very little has changed in this regard throughout my entire forty-year dance with cancer.

Anna sees the silver lining of each situation, believing every challenge often has an upside. For example, being forced to take time off work for treatments allowed Anna to spend more time at home with her daughter. Her house explosion led to a new home with brand-new appliances.

Asked how she has endured, Anna responds: "The Lord has truly blessed me. I'm sure I have an archangel as my guardian angel . . . and he has been sorely tested to keep me going!

"Even if I die, I still win. My greatest wish is to go to heaven. Dying would give me this wish," she says, laughing, "though some people might think I'm going somewhere else. And I would have no more pain or suffering."

Anna stays busy doing things she loves, which feeds her soul and gives her energy. She has published several books, all available on Amazon.com. *Anna's Journey: How Many Lives Does One Person Get?*, *Anna's Journey: Am I Accident Prone?*, and *Anna's Journey: My 40 Year Dance with Cancer* are all memoirs. She has written two children's books about cancer, she created the "Mitzy the Butterfly" series to raise children's awareness about the environment, and she has written a few other books just for fun.

Anna began hosting an Internet radio show, "Anna's Journey," in 2011. She likes to write poetry, is the editorial columnist for her local paper, and does freelance reporting. She is also a grandmother of three.

Anna also makes time to advocate for cancer care and to volunteer for her church, the Cancer Support Foundation, American Cancer Society, Baltimore County Cancer Coalition, and her local hospital. She is a member of the Our Lady of Mt. Carmel Parish Council and its school board, as well as a member of the Patient Safety Advisory Board of MedStar Franklin Square Medical Center.

Asked how she finds time for all of this, Anna says she uses her time wisely and simply does what she can, when she can. "Why sit here and do nothing?" she asks. After all, she says, God must have a reason for her still being alive.

In the foreword to *Anna's Journey: How Many Lives Does One Person Get?,* Anna's friend Ginny Robertson elaborates:

> While Anna is a cancer survivor, she has never been a cancer victim. I've seen others fall prey to the diagnosis of a gloomy physician or be one who can't face yet another chemo treatment or medication side effect. Anna seems to find the joy in being alive to face these things. And in all the years I've known her, her medical challenges have never gotten in the way of her desire to help others.

Anna dedicated *Anna's Journey: My 40 Year Dance with Cancer* to "all who have traveled the path of cancer... Patients, Caregivers, Providers, Family & Friends..." Often, she writes, dealing with serious medical conditions like cancer can be a catalyst for positive change. She shares her experiences with cancer to give others hope.

"I know my resilience, which I have gathered to weather these experiences, has also been a source of strength for many who have crossed my path, giving them hope and the awareness to reach deeply for their own talents and gifts for survival," Anna writes.

Anna urges those with cancer to keep a journal so they can share every little symptom with their doctor, because sometimes the smallest detail is the most important. "Too many people do not recognize what their 'good' feels like or recognize when it begins to change," she states. "People make excuses, fearing a serious illness would be diagnosed, just like I did."

She highly recommends finding doctors you trust and who listen to you. Always get a second opinion. Do your research so you can ask the right questions.

Perhaps most importantly, be vigilant and act quickly:

> Early detection has been my pet project for the last thirty years or more. It is probably the No. 1 reason I have survived cancer eight different times. I strongly urge everyone to get the necessary screenings *and* to be very aware of your own body. Be ready to admit when something does not seem right. Do not hesitate to visit the doctor to have something checked.

Grateful to be where she is today, Anna knows life can change in an instant. She says she is doing "relatively well." "Technically, I'm dying from metastatic breast cancer," Anna says, laughing, "but I'm up and active!"

Anna believes she has survived so many scares because of great medical care and her strong belief in God. She is a model of faith, courage, optimism, and perseverance. "I am a thriving cancer survivor," she says. "A positive attitude, early detection, and my faith in God have gotten me through tough times."

Until a cure is found, Anna Renault will continue to write books and live life to the fullest, helping others along the way, and refusing to live in fear of another bout with cancer. She says:

> This forty-year journey is responsible for making me a strong, resilient, spirited, and perhaps even a bit pushy woman who goes full tilt until illness slows me down. Yes, it has slowed me down for a couple of weeks or sometimes for a year or two, but it has not stopped me…at least not yet!

...................................................................

You can learn more about Anna Renault at annarenault. com. If you would like to make a donation in her honor, please do so at cancersupportfoundation.org.

# Sara Beth

Sara Beth Vaughn might be one of the most upbeat people in America. Despite being diagnosed with spastic cerebral palsy as an infant, she sees this "disability" as a blessing and has dedicated her life to helping others.

"I tend to stand out among a crowd, go against the grain," Sara Beth says. "Whichever way you choose to word it, I'm just a plain 'outside of the box' woman."

Spastic cerebral palsy is a developmental disorder caused by damage to the brain before or during birth or within the first few years of life. Spastic CP is the most common type of cerebral palsy, frequently characterized by muscle and joint stiffness and erratic movements. "However," Sara Beth says, "living with CP has served as the largest blessing in my life to date!"

In her manuscript *Perspective: Does CP Stand for Cerebral Palsy or…Compassion?*, which she hopes to turn into a book, she explains:

> You see, I am what most folks would often describe as "disabled." I was diagnosed with having spastic cerebral palsy at the ripe old age of eighteen months. I believe we are what we think. With this in mind, I often refer to myself as "experiencing living life with CP" or "experiencing a physical handicap."

At thirty years old, Sara Beth says her life has had both challenges and empowering triumphs. She focuses more on the latter and believes pain and suffering can be used for the greater good.

Sara Beth puts forth a challenge in *Perspective*:

> Life is hard, but it tends to be much more of a challenge when we feel that no one is in our corner. Each day, let's set a goal to serve as that support for at least one individual, if they will have us. Supporting one another is the key. I often find that I serve myself by serving others! Try boosting someone's spirits tomorrow and see if your own spirits aren't boosted by the process as well!

Her motivation for writing her story is to inspire others. Our tests give us wisdom, she says, "so we would be remiss to keep silent regarding the valuable insights we have learned through enduring and triumphing over our unique struggles along the way."

Sara Beth believes that when we start seeing our differences as attributes that make us extraordinary, real growth can occur. When we learn to accept ourselves as we truly are, we can positively affect others as well.

Everything happens for a reason, a valuable purpose, she says. Opening up to others in turn helps us offer compassion. "Showing compassion is often the first step in restoring hope," Sara Beth writes, "and without hope, it can become a bit more challenging to put our feet on the ground with purpose upon waking."

Due to Sara Beth's physical constraints as a toddler, the medical field placed limits on Sara Beth very early on—she'd never do this or be able to accomplish that. Because she was able to prove them wrong so many times, Sara Beth is compelled to help others shatter their perceived ceilings. She has devoted her life to giving hope to others, to assisting them in conquering unfair labels. Her definition of happiness is reaching "all who long for the weight of oppression to be lifted from their chests."

Sara Beth was born three and a half months premature on August 13, 1987, at St. Mary's Hospital in Evansville, Indiana. She weighed 1.7 pounds.

Tiny Sara Beth was put in an incubator, dependent upon a staggering number of machines to live. She writes:

> Being as substantially premature as I was, my eyelids were translucent, and my fingernails and toenails had yet to form. The lungs of my tiny little body were so underdeveloped that they were unable to breathe without assistance. Within twenty-four hours of living, my heart had already ceased to beat three times. Doctors weren't hopeful, as they explained to my parents that *if* their daughter survived another day, she would know nothing more than a life in a vegetative state—never know herself, nor her parents, and remain bed- or wheelchair-bound for all of her days.

Three blood clots were detected in the center of Sara Beth's brain within seventy-two hours of her birth. Doctors asked her parents whether blood transfusions, necessary for the baby's survival, should continue. Sara Beth's parents didn't hesitate; they wanted every measure possible taken to allow their daughter to live.

Their resolve paid off, Sara Beth writes:

> A few weeks later, doctors were stunned when the three blood clots squatting in my brain diminished, as if by magic, without causing any further brain damage. We all knew it was not magic. It was the BIG GUY UPSTAIRS!

The miracle baby spent the first three months of her life in the newborn intensive care unit. When she was finally sent home, Sara Beth was tethered to a heart monitor.

Anyone who babysat Sara Beth had to be CPR-certified. Her "Papaw" was her most frequent babysitter. He, along with the rest of her family, taught Sara Beth that true happiness comes from working for a cause bigger than oneself.

Papaw, Sara Beth's kind and gentle grandpa Larry, was a special friend. When he was eight years old, a farming accident had severely damaged his legs. His own physical limitations led to a deep bond between him and his granddaughter.

"My grandpa's physical pains, challenges, and suffering led him to play the part of a leading advocate early on in my childhood," Sara Beth remembers. "He taught me that a broken lamp can be glued back together, and even with the scar of a fracture, that lamp still contributes an abundance of light to the world."

When Sara Beth was diagnosed with cerebral palsy, she couldn't crawl or sit up on her own, let alone stand or walk. Despite her developmental hold-ups, Sara Beth writes that she had an early talent:

> One of the things I learned to do right away... talking! You see, when you have a child who lacks the ability to physically get up and get what they need, they learn to verbally convey to their caregivers what it is they need in accommodation for physical barriers. And that is exactly what I did! I began speaking full sentences by the time I was one year old, and I haven't been able to close my mouth since!

Sara Beth walked exclusively on her tiptoes as a child. She was severely pigeon-toed, and her left leg was longer than her right. She also had scoliosis.

Fortunately for Sara Beth, a local group of Hadi Shriners stepped in to cover expenses for medical assessments, screenings, and procedures. They sent her to Shriners Hospitals for Children in St. Louis, Missouri, where Sara Beth had eight surgeries between the ages of three and eighteen, mostly before she was five. The Shriners' generosity is responsible for fixing most of Sara Beth's lower-body issues.

The staff at Shriners Hospital provided exceptional care, making the children feel special and in safe hands. After some of her surgeries, Sara Beth stayed at the hospital for a few days; after others, she remained for months. Most procedures were scheduled in the summer to prevent her from missing school. One of her parents stayed with Sara Beth each time.

During inpatient care, the kids at the hospital attended group physical therapy. "It was there that the real magic took place," Sara Beth says. "I am talking about recovery and relearning how to walk in a sense, but more than that, the real lesson was that we all learned to see each other for who we actually were."

Despite her frequent hospital stays and having to spend months in casts from her neck to her toes, Sara Beth says she wouldn't trade her childhood for anything. Her experiences gave her "the capacity to look beyond the superficiality of human nature to see people for who they truly are. It is very important that we all try to refrain from making judgments about what a person can or cannot do until they actually start speaking to us. [That] is probably my most prized lesson I have learned throughout my life.

"Embracing our differences as attributes gives us our 'edge,' that which sets us apart from our peers and colleagues. Normalcy is ultimately just a figment of our imagination... The way I see it, we all fall on the 'spectrum of crazy' somewhere. Challenges are opportunities to personally grow and develop if we can find the insights to gain within each hard aspect."

By age five, Sara Beth learned to walk with a walker. But when six-year-old Sara Beth entered her first-grade classroom, she noticed none of the other kids used a walker. That idea was new to her; until then, she'd never felt there was anything wrong with her.

To fit in, Sara Beth decided she didn't need her walker anymore. Worried about her safety, the school called her parents. Sara Beth's mother responded: "Sara Beth is strong. Let her fall. She will learn."

That tough-love approach and Sara Beth's stubborn determination forced Sara Beth's body to learn to walk without support. Her family and the Shriners trained Sara Beth that there was no such thing as "you can't do this." She gives them credit for making her into the woman she is today. "The English language does not even have appropriate verbiage to convey how full my heart is due to all the blessings I have had in my life," she says.

But Sara Beth knows firsthand how easy it can be to spiral into "Why me?" thinking.

In 2012, Sara Beth had just completed a master's degree in social work at the University of Southern Indiana. She got a full-time nonprofit job, leased a new vehicle, and moved into her first apartment. But when she came home one day, everything of value she owned had been stolen by an untrustworthy partner.

She admits to throwing herself a pity party: *I've already been through so much. Why, God, would you let me be subjected to something as horrendous as this?* But she soon picked herself back up, realizing she didn't want to wallow in a victim mindset any longer. She explains:

> Quite honestly, being burglarized was the best possible thing that could have happened to me— for two reasons.
>
> 1. It served as the catapult I needed to get myself out of a bad relationship, which has further provided me with insights on how to better support and guide those who are currently experiencing a similar situation.
>
> 2. God and I both know I am a stubborn lady. Thus, He knew that was the only way I would learn the hard lesson that nothing that is actually tangible to our touch holds any real value whatsoever. I didn't even replace half of what was stolen from me once I regained my footing from that traumatic experience. It seems to me now that the less you have, the less you have to worry about. I am going to have to thank God with a bear hug when I see Him for teaching me this lesson so early in life.

After the theft, Sara Beth threw herself into her work. She followed her own advice, putting the focus on serving others. Helping and inspiring others accelerated her transformation from victim to survivor.

For the past four years, the five-foot-tall ball of energy has been an assessment specialist at a nonprofit, working to prevent and end homelessness in the Evansville area. Sara Beth is an advocate for at-risk individuals, directing people to services, programs, and housing options to get those in need back on their feet. She is ecstatic to get paid for doing her dream job.

Sara Beth has many roles, but the most important to her is restoring people's hope. She says her ability to express herself early in life has led to her serving on the board of directors for a local family shelter. Sara Beth says she is skilled in making people laugh, often because of her lack of a filter. "For the last thirty years, I've just gotten louder," she says.

She is committed to raising awareness for Shriners, whose organization supports children and their families. Wanting to give back, Sara Beth has been a guest speaker at Shriners Hospitals events, sharing how the Shriners' generosity and compassion changed her life. She also has volunteered for the local Hadi Shrine center's fundraisers.

Sara Beth shares the power of positive thinking with corporations, universities, prisons, shelters, and groups as a motivational speaker. She loves talking to groups, noting that when you've stood out in life since day one, any fear of speaking in front of others goes away quickly. Sara Beth has made something of a name for herself in southwest Indiana. "Every life event I have been honored to experience from birth up to this very present moment has culminated in this beautiful, destined reality that I currently find myself within," she says.

Sara Beth is an example of what can happen when negative thinking is surmounted. Despite being labeled abnormal and disabled, Sara Beth sees her distinctions as a miracle:

> If people remember you, most often they also remember the causes you stand for. I enjoy that people can pick me out of a crowd, because hopefully it reminds them of what I hold as value in my affiliations: everyone is connected, we all deserve support and compassion, and we are what we think—meaning that if you believe in yourself, you can manifest in your life whatever you can dream up!
>
> Every day I am humbled to meet new people, hear their stories, and learn vicariously through them the lessons that it may have taken them years of hardship to master. The truth is, from the moment we are born, we have within us everything we need in order to become who we were always meant to be.

Sara Beth loves to show people their own abilities:

> The extraordinary moment of transcendence takes place when the words "you can" transform into the empowering statement of "I can." This particular moment of pure inspiration I have been fortunate enough to witness. It is so completely life-altering to witness the uncanny change from heartbreaking

despair into something of pure empowerment, strength, and self-advocacy. That is my reason for being.

Sara Beth believes we can all find happiness in who we are. We have an inherent ability to grow, to change. She tries to see the best in people and to better herself every day.

From first receiving hope from the Shriners to now passing it on to others, Sara Beth says she is humbled to realize her life has come full circle:

I am proud of myself. Be proud of yourself. Let's be proud together.

Don't forget that you are the only you. You have something unique to contribute! My experience of living with a physical handicap has revealed to me that I can contribute compassion in my own unique way.

I encourage you to see that in the end, we are all very much connected! Once someone has inspired the restoration of hope in your life or assisted you in overcoming any variety of adversity, you then are qualified to do the same for another. This concept is the motivation behind who I am and what I stand for today, which in essence is helping others to believe and know that they are whoever they want to be. We are not obligated to become who society says we are. It brings me joy to share my story with one person or 10,000 people. I will speak to anyone who is willing to lend me their ear. Remember, you do not have to have initials behind your name to make a positive impact on someone's life. All you need in order to manifest such an act of kindness is compassion.

...................................................................

If you would like to make a donation in honor of Sara Beth, please do so at ozanamfamilyshelter.org.

# Todd

When Todd Crandell did his first line of cocaine in his school's parking lot, he instantly thought he'd found what he'd been looking for, the drug that would fix everything.

Though he was one of the best hockey players in the state of Ohio as a high school senior, Todd searched desperately for something to fill the emptiness he felt inside.

That quest would take him on a decade-long journey of addiction that ultimately led him to the most unexpected of destinations: heading an addiction-recovery program and achieving status as a world-renowned triathlete.

Todd's pain began early in life. When he was three years old, his mother committed suicide after struggling with addiction. She was in her early twenties. "Her leaving me just caused this big, gaping wound in me, and I didn't understand emotionally why I was the way I was," Todd says. "I wanted to know why I hated myself so much, why I felt I wasn't good enough."

His father says Todd thought his mother's death was somehow his fault. His mom's suicide created an emotional void, leaving Todd a lost kid with no self-respect or self-esteem. Todd started drinking at the age of thirteen and tried cocaine at sixteen.

Caught doing cocaine on the team bus, Todd got kicked off the hockey team. His downward spiral of abusing liquor, coke, heroin, and crack led to him being thrown in jail multiple times. He ultimately became homeless, living out of his car. Todd had serious thoughts about committing suicide. He figured he'd have the same fate as his mother and didn't care if he lived or died, thinking, *OK, let's get this over with.*

On April 15, 1993, after his third DUI, Todd put his beer down. He said to himself, "That's it. This is over. I'm going to put my life back together."

He quit drugs and alcohol cold turkey. Todd began playing hockey again, enrolled in college, and attended recovery meetings. "The same tenacity that I put into destroying myself, I just needed to switch it and put it into repairing myself," he says.

He redirected his energy to a new aspiration: completing an Ironman triathlon. The Ironman is a grueling endurance race. Participants swim 2.4 miles, bike 112 miles, and run 26.2 miles. In one day. In other words, the triathletes swim and bike a tremendously long way *before* running a marathon.

When Todd puts his mind to doing something, whether it's deciding to quit abusing drugs and alcohol or completing an Ironman, he is going to do it. Todd knows people say he has just switched addictions, but he says his intense training is more a focus than an addiction. On November 6, 1999,

Todd completed his first Ironman race.

In an interview with Channel 9 Australia ("From Addict to Ironman"), Todd says police that used to arrest him and even former party friends contacted him when they heard about his miraculous turnaround. As he transformed mentally, physically, and emotionally, Todd decided he wanted to help others battling addiction.

Though he supports twelve-step programs, after a year or two of trying them himself, Todd wanted something more. In 2001, he founded Racing for Recovery™, a federally approved 501(c)(3) nonprofit organization with a mission "to prevent all forms of substance abuse by promoting a lifestyle of fitness and health for all those affected by addiction." His program differs from traditional options, focusing on fitness and involving family and close friends in the treatment.

Todd went back to school to get a master's degree and became a licensed professional clinical counselor and licensed independent chemical dependency counselor. Todd helps clients understand the emotional traumas that led to their drug addictions. The objective is for clients to heal their traumas while practicing a holistic lifestyle.

Todd's story got attention, including a ten-and-a-half-minute feature on ESPN in the spring of 2007. Introduced by late ESPN anchor Stuart Scott, the touching "Addict to Ironman" story by reporter Tom Rinaldi brought Todd's mission into living rooms worldwide. Todd, then forty years old, wasn't prepared for the blitz of calls after the piece aired. Four phone lines had to be installed to handle the onslaught.

With drug addiction and overdoses currently at epidemic levels in America, Todd finds himself constantly busy. His program is full of clients trying to get clean and sober. Todd is determined "to just give them a glimmer of hope of what's in front of them and say, 'You can have this. Let me show you how to get it.'"

The Racing for Recovery website explains that the organization "offers a unique, cutting-edge, holistic model for treating addiction." The organization firmly believes in including close friends and family in the process: "Family members are encouraged to share how addiction has impacted them. Racing for Recovery has recognized that when all points of view are shared in a structured setting, everyone is able to heal."

Racing for Recovery held its fifteenth annual 5k/10k run/walk event on October 30, 2016, on the campus of Lourdes University in Sylvania, Ohio. The event's purpose, in addition to celebrating fifteen years of changing and saving lives, was "to help promote awareness, prevention, and treatment for everyone affected by substance abuse." Prior to the event, Todd said: "Gratitude and humility have enabled me to attain and sustain sobriety. I want to help that occur in others, and the annual run/walk is another perfect opportunity to share this gift."

In addition to the 5k/10k, the organization hosts a

half-marathon as well as fitness gatherings, and sponsors a softball team. "These signature events bring together struggling and recovering addicts, family, friends, volunteers, everyday athletes, sponsors, donors, supporters, and the entire community to enjoy the outdoors, get fresh air, exercise, and see that with sobriety, anything is possible," Todd says. Racing for Recovery also offers professional counseling, intensive outpatient services, intervention services, motivational speaking, a mentoring program, and a live online support group.

In one-on-one and group counseling, the Racing for Recovery team tries to get to the root of a client's addiction, whether that be the death of a loved one, divorce, physical or sexual abuse, or any other catalyst. Todd believes substance abusers can end dependence on drugs and alcohol once they understand why emotional traumas control them.

According to its website, Racing for Recovery holds several weekly support group meetings open to "men and women of all ages, education levels and backgrounds, recovering addicts, their friends and family, students, volunteers, community leaders, business owners and athletes— all of whom, whether personally affected by addiction or otherwise, notice its negative impact and want to be part of a movement to promote change and positive alternatives within their communities." Family interventions offer a compassionate, non-combative environment to help with the most extreme crisis situations.

Todd shares his experiences by speaking in schools, businesses, jails and detention centers, and drug treatment facilities nationwide.

At one time hooked on drugs and alcohol and living in his car, Todd has turned his life around to become an elite athlete. He has completed twenty-eight Ironman triathlons in fifteen countries on six continents. The Racing for Recovery website goes on: "In 2008, he completed the Ultraman Hawaii, a grueling three-day endurance test [swim 6.2 miles and bike 90 miles on day one, ride 172 miles on day two, and run 52 miles—basically a double-marathon—on day three] followed six days later by another Ironman in Western Australia. In 2009 he completed Ultraman Canada and became one of 25 people worldwide to complete both Ultraman events."

Now twenty-three years sober, Todd has been married for twenty years and has four kids. He turned fifty on December 12, 2016. Though busy being an attentive husband, a productive and present father, and leading Racing for Recovery, Todd says his life is all about finding balance.

A licensed counselor, Todd says clients relate to him due to his own personal battle with substance abuse. One client shares, "I can relate to Todd's counseling methods because he has lived through the same thing I am. I see where his life is today and realize there is a life without drugs. I want it."

Todd has helped thousands of addicts through his unique approach to recovery. Focusing on a holistic lifestyle, education, physical and mental health, spirituality, volunteerism, and giving back to the community, many clients are now sober, gainfully employed, and productive members of society. Racing for Recovery is funded by donations, sales from two books Todd has co-written (*Racing for Recovery: From Addict to Ironman* with John Hanc and *There's More Than One Way to Get to Cleveland* with Tim Vandehey), money from insurance companies, and a few sponsors.

Giving hope to those who are lost and don't think they can recover is Todd's life purpose, but his mission has its own challenges. As he told ESPN:

> I've lost everything. Cars repossessed, house been in foreclosure three different times. I've questioned sometimes, *Have I done the right thing? In trying to help other people, have I lost my family? Have I sacrificed my family to help that addict?* And, at times, I have.

Because of the time he spent launching Racing for Recovery, Todd was fired from a white-collar career in the pharmaceutical industry. While at a Racing for Recovery golf fundraiser one day, his wife called saying the electric company was going to shut off the electricity at their home if the couple didn't act fast. The Crandell family even lost its house, but Todd was undeterred; he had risen to the occasion before. He knew his calling in life, so he found a way to make his dream happen.

If anything, he says, overcoming these obstacles just shows his tenacity and dedication. "And now I feel like I made it," he says. "It was worth it."

Even after Todd decided to live sober, he continued to have suicidal thoughts and was in a dark place for many years. He had a lot of pain, deep depression, and rage to face. Only in the past few years have those demons left his side. "The emotional hurt that made me *choose* to use was the real problem, not the drugs," he explains. Surprisingly, Todd has never been tempted to use drugs since the day he quit. He was done and hasn't looked back.

The Racing for Recovery founder survived an addiction that "cost me everything." Todd lost his family, friends, and himself. "I could have been a pro hockey player, and I pissed it away because of drugs," he admits. "I was on something basically twenty-four hours a day. I could not figure out how to live without drugs. And I couldn't figure out how to stop them."

Once he got sober, Todd played semi-pro hockey for ten years. After proving to himself he had legitimate talent, he hung up his skates to focus on education and Racing for Recovery.

At first, Todd replaced the high from drugs and alcohol with the high of finishing an extreme race. These days, he gets as much of a high helping others overcome addiction.

When it comes to recovery, "choice" is his favorite word. Todd candidly admits he once chose to live under the influence but now chooses to live sober, and he's worked tirelessly to build a better life. Todd is grateful for the help he's received from many others, but he says all big, positive change starts from within. After seeing thousands of clients, Todd believes transformation often comes down to self-esteem; many users simply do not value themselves.

Though he has been featured by major news outlets such as ESPN and *USA Today*, among others, Todd says empathy, humility, and gratitude are his foundation. The Racing for Recovery program is about relating to one another, rather than comparing. Whereas traditional programs take place in a stable environment and then release people right back into the same situation they came from, Todd says of Racing for Recovery, "It's not just another rehab; it's a lifestyle."

Todd wants his own kids to see "the dangers of addiction and the success of sobriety." To be a good example, he takes responsibility for his past, tries to improve himself in the present, and prepares for the future. Todd reminds his children they wouldn't be here if he'd continued with his addiction.

He is far more proud of himself for pursuing his passion, for helping people, for his marriage, and for being a good parent than for any of his athletic achievements. Though being one of the thirty people chosen from around the world to compete in an Ultraman competition is quite an honor, Todd says the people whom fellow competitors and fans relate to and respect aren't necessarily the most amazing athletes, but those who give credit to their support network and overcome major obstacles to participate in the first place.

Another source of price for Todd: Racing for Recovery's sixteen-thousand-square-foot facility that opened September 1, 2016. Two hundred twenty-two people showed up on opening night. The building houses support group meetings, intensive outpatient groups, individual counseling, board meetings, a gym, kitchen, spirituality room, and computer room. Every Thursday night, around a hundred people come to the facility for group meetings, and there are twelve to fifteen individuals in intensive outpatient groups each week, plus about fifteen one-on-one clients.

Todd discussed his distinctive approach to treating addiction in a piece that appeared in the *Los Angeles Times* in November 2016:

> People don't just stop using drugs or alcohol because somebody tells them to. They need to be presented with something new that shows them the positive benefits of coming off addiction. We don't just focus on not using drugs, but also...living a happy, productive lifestyle.

Todd has the boundless energy and drive of a characteristic leader. He is the founder of the organization but has an executive director that "works with me, not for me." Todd emphasizes the focus is not on his own accomplishments, but on helping as many people as possible. Securing a twelve-bedroom live-in complex two miles from the main facility is Todd's next goal.

Racing for Recovery participants aren't sitting around in front of a TV. They train six days a week; they're in the pool at 6 a.m., running by 9 a.m., and riding bikes in the afternoon. Though no one is expected to complete an Ironman, some of his clients have done exactly that. "Racing for Recovery is a program of action," Todd explains. "We physically get fit, we spiritually get fit, we emotionally get fit, and we apply those things to not only help ourselves, but to help someone else."

He believes that if those in recovery put the same effort into bettering themselves that they once devoted to destroying themselves, they can stay sober. "But that's the beauty of the journey in this whole thing," he says. "It's overcoming the struggles, it's building the support system, it's giving back and helping someone else—that's the rush of sustaining that sobriety. That's what I'm in this for. I love it."

Those recovering still have struggles, but they are improving. That's what the Racing for Recovery program is all about. One might say that's what life is all about, too.

Todd says: "Just like with my addiction, one was never enough, and helping one person is not enough for me either. If I can help one and this program can help one, we can help a thousand, and if we can help a thousand, we can help ten thousand. And so it goes on and on and on."

If Todd Crandell says he's going to do something, it's a good bet he will.

....................................................................

If you would like to make a donation in honor of Todd
Crandell, please do so at racingforrecovery.org.

# Stacey

Instead of giving up on her marriage, Stacey Greene confronted the pain and humiliation of infidelity head on. She and her husband worked hard to save their relationship, a path many people avoid. Though she wrote her book *Stronger Than Broken—One couple's decision to move through an affair* as a fictional story, she says the account is ninety-eight percent autobiographical.

Stacey met her husband, "Jim," at a restaurant in the 1980s when she overheard him say he, too, was vegetarian. Though Stacey was six years younger, the two found they'd grown up in the same neighborhood in northeast Ohio and were both runners. After a year, they were entering the same races and moved in together. They married and had twin boys, another boy, and then a girl.

Stacey played many sports as a youth, and as an adult, she tried to remain as active as her stressful life allowed. Yet Stacey admits, "Three boys and one girl in just under seven years takes a toll on the body, the romance, and the time we had for each other."

The kids became involved in sports, music, and clubs, straining the couple's time together. By the 1990s, life gave the couple additional challenges, as Stacey's father had

Alzheimer's and Jim's mom suffered the first of three heart attacks. Soon the couple slept in separate rooms.

"I love yous" became rare. Shared runs gave way to "running the kids here and there, trying to see each band concert, game played, swim meet, or award that was presented," Stacey recalls. Date nights diminished and Jim retreated to his "man cave" in the basement more and more, even for dinner. Arguments over finances and free time became common. Stacey doesn't know what kept them together during the "ugly years."

Still, they decided to renew their vows in August 2011 on their twenty-fifth wedding anniversary. The celebration was a huge hit. Stacey had a great time, proud they had reached the milestone together. However, their life had become mundane; often, date nights amounted to sitting on the couch watching TV or movies.

By the time the twins went away to college, Stacey started working a retail job until 11 p.m. to help pay the double tuitions, while also working her daytime jobs as a caregiver and a youth sports coach. She understood Jim's "guy time" with his friends. "Couples need to have their own friends and keep their own identities," Stacey says. After all, she enjoyed occasional nights out with girlfriends. The difference was that Jim's nights out lasted until the wee hours of the morning.

Stacey typically fell asleep in the family room, waiting to hear her husband's key in the front door. She often stayed on the couch for the night once Jim had come home, but one night she went up to the bedroom. When she walked into the room, Jim quickly slid his cell phone under the sheets.

Caught red-handed, Jim reluctantly admitted he'd been texting and seeing a forty-one-year-old single mother. They'd met at a bar four or five months earlier. Completely blindsided by the affair, Stacey got lightheaded. As the truth sank in, she sobbed uncontrollably until she fell asleep, exhausted.

When she awoke, she found a letter. "I know it was selfish, and I tried to stop; it was all about feeling young again, and it was addicting," Jim confessed. "I couldn't turn it off. I know it was wrong and selfish, and she tried to stop too, but we couldn't."

Sad and angry, Stacey called her pastor to make an appointment for consolation and advice, but he was out of town. She couldn't eat for the next few days. "I was determined to stay somewhat functional for the kids, who still seemed oblivious to what issues Mom and Dad were having," she says.

Stacey tried to put on a good game face at work, too, waiting to put on her makeup until after she'd stopped crying in the parking lot. After four days of Stacey not eating, a coworker spoke up about Stacey's wan appearance, which she played off as the effects of a juice cleanse. Knowing she needed to talk to someone, Stacey swallowed her pride and called her sister. She prayed a lot but still had trouble sleeping, even having nightmares, "before the alarm jolted me back into another crappy day as the wife of a cheating bastard."

Eventually, she looked through Jim's phone and was flabbergasted to find more than four hundred text messages to his mistress. Stacey couldn't help herself from reading every single one. Her snooping uncovered that Jim and the woman had indeed had sex.

"I know it seems so junior high school, but I was completely jealous of this woman and the power she had over my husband to turn him into a lovesick boy again," Stacey acknowledges. She thought maybe she was at fault; picking up a second job to earn extra money for the family was time she should have spent with her husband. For this reason—and because she didn't trust Jim alone on Friday and Saturday nights while she worked—Stacey put in her two weeks' notice at her night job.

In her book, Stacey shares:

> I was cheated on. I was lied to. Yes, omission of
> truth is also a lie in my book. I am trying so hard
> to be normal and put this all behind me. It simply
> isn't that easy knowing that somehow, in some way,
> I did not measure up to keeping Jim faithful and
> loyal to me. How is it that I had no idea?

A sermon by the associate pastor at her church during this time seemed to be aimed directly at Stacey. He spoke about forgiveness, which got Stacey thinking. She made a concerted effort to forgive Jim. Stacey also found it in her heart to forgive the woman, trying to understand what raising a child as a single mother at the age of forty-one might be like.

Still angry, humiliated, and not wanting pity from friends and family, Stacey kept the secret to herself. To his credit, Jim went to counseling with Stacey's pastor when he got back into town. The pastor talked to the couple together and then individually. When he asked what the couple wanted to do, a long pause ended with Jim saying, "Fix it." (The couple had tried traditional marriage counseling for other issues years earlier but got nothing out of it. Aside from the two visits with the pastor, rebuilding their relationship would be "on our own with our stubbornness and determination," Stacey says.)

Stacey remained paranoid and insecure, however. Unable to fight the urge, she looked the woman up on Facebook after doing some investigating to find her name. The woman lived within fifteen miles of Stacey's family. Jim's text messages played "like a broken record in my brain."

As Stacey writes:

> I run on the treadmill or venture out into the rainy spring and run until I am spent. I listen to sad love songs in some feeble attempt to know that I am not the only one feeling this pain. I try to appear happy and normal for the kids, but I am still not eating like I used to. I mope around. I don't enjoy going to work and faking a smile. I follow my husband around from room to room when he is home, as

if I still need to see what he is doing every waking minute. My pathetic mind is still thinking that if he is spending the time with me, then he can't be spending it with her or anyone else.

But she still loved her husband. Even Jim didn't understand why Stacey still cared for him after what he'd done and what he'd put her through. Stacey went eleven days before finally eating a solid meal. At a family funeral, Jim's mother even commented on how drained Stacey looked, asking why she ate so little at the meal.

To move forward, Stacey recalled an incident from her past. As a young girl, Stacey had broken her arm in a bike accident. Though her mom was terrified, the doctor reassured them that often the healed area of injury is stronger than before the incident. Stacey believed the same could happen with her relationship.

To fix their marriage, Stacey and Jim quickly learned a lot of work would be involved. They knew they must greatly improve their communication. Jim agreed to read several marriage and relationship books with his wife. Stacey asked him to help her healing process by being more physically and emotionally present, by spending quality time with her, and by giving her more hugs and direct eye contact. "We were confronted with the realization that we took a lot of things for granted," she admits. "We forgot how to talk about anything other than bills and the kids…We even realized that we spoke different love languages."

Stacey continued to be overcome by tidal waves of sadness despite the increased attention Jim showed her and their once-a-week date nights. She distracted herself with baking, exercise, and music. Their communication was improving, however, and they learned to be more open and honest with one another. They began focusing more on their friendship and less on their roles as parents and spouses.

Wanting to help others, Stacey decided to write about her recovery from infidelity in her book. Pouring her heart out for the book was therapeutic for Stacey, and she hopes her honesty will assist others in similar circumstances.

Stacey has been journaling her entire life. She is currently working on another book, *Stronger With Love*, a handbook for couples struggling with all sorts of issues, not just infidelity. The book will tell multiple stories of others overcoming serious life challenges and is meant to give people comfort.

Her third book probably will be *Letters to the Dead Men*, a book about the gratitude she feels toward several key male figures in her life, each of whom taught her valuable lessons. Excluding her husband and son, every significant man Stacey has known—including her grandfather, father, two brothers, and two friends from high school—all died before she could thank them for the positive impact they had on her life. Stacey wants to use the book to show her appreciation and properly say goodbye.

*Stronger Than Broken* includes song lyrics and Bible passages and has gotten excellent reviews on Amazon. "I do not profess to be a psychologist, counselor, or expert in relationships," Stacey says. "I am just like many of you, trying to juggle the demands of motherhood, career, daughter, and wife."

Stacey readily confesses that she began writing her first book for the wrong reasons. She originally wanted to hand the book to the woman involved in her husband's affair, but then she thought better of choosing the revenge route. Stacey could hear her father speaking to her from beyond the grave, saying she'd been raised better. Instead, her book's purpose became more about healing and moving on.

She writes:

> With God's grace, we saved our own marriage. It was not easy. It was genuine work as we prayed, spoke to the pastor, and used some great relationship books to prompt us. It was a struggle to uncover the judgment and blame. It was genuine effort to recommit to each other on paper as well as in our hearts. But we made that choice—together… we were able to move through this. With our decision and intention to save this marriage, I don't feel that we will ever intentionally hurt each other, stray, or take each other for granted again. I think we will always remember the pain of the last year but seek to live in the present moment.

*Stronger Than Broken* deals with infidelity and the resulting emotions, but it is also about forgiveness, healing, and love.

Despite a national divorce rate at fifty percent, not many people are willing to talk about this all-too-common issue.

Stacey points out, "It is so much easier for couples to throw away the marriage like an old pair of running shoes when things get difficult, and then they blame each other for their own unhappiness." She suggests partners need to remember the good times but work to make new memories. Couples must remember their children will use the example they set for their own relationships. "Leave a legacy that you can be proud of," Stacey says.

With wisdom gained only by experience, Stacey says: "Each relationship needs a makeover every now and then. Spouses can learn from each other and continue to grow together as a couple if each one is willing to share in the other's life." She believes the affair was put in her life to shake her to the core and give her marriage a fresh start.

Recommitted to full disclosure in their marriage, Stacey wrestled with how to tell her husband about her book. She prayed for guidance and summoned the courage. Jim was okay with the book so long as he got to be the first reader and Stacey changed their names. (Stacey refers to herself as "Michelle" in her book.) "Thank God we evolved past the ugly years," Stacey says.

Stacey and her husband have waited to discuss the dark days of their relationship with their children. Stacey is unsure how much their children know, but she does believe her youngest child knew something was amiss because of Stacey's many nights of loud sobbing in the room directly upstairs. Now that the kids are close to being adults themselves, Stacey and her husband plan to bring the truth into the open.

Stacey talks to groups of all kinds about her experiences to give people a positive alternative, believing that helping prevent premature divorces is her calling. The divorce rate and the quickness with which couples give up on marriage greatly saddens Stacey. Unlike many people, Stacey believes arguing and making up in front of children is a healthy example for today's youth (as long as the fighting is non-physical). After all, disagreements are part of the human condition.

Now five years removed from the tough times, Stacey writes:

> We talk openly, we fight less, we make real eye contact, we smile at each other more, we make an effort to include the other one in decisions, and we are exploring new and often crazy ways to please each other. We are not perfect, but we are not broken. Yes, that's what Jimmy and I are now... stronger than broken.

Love can hurt, but true love lasts.

...........................................................................

If you would like to make a donation in honor of Stacey Greene, please do so to Alive On Purpose, a nonprofit dedicated to the promotion of life by finding help for people struggling with depression, trauma, and suicide (imaliveonpurpose.org).

# Mick

At the beginning of Leslie "Mick" Ebeling's fascinating book *Not Impossible: The Art and Joy of Doing What Couldn't Be Done*, Mick quotes Henry Ford: "Whether you think you can, or think you can't, you're right." Mick is definitely someone who believes he can accomplish any goal—and that has led to life-changing innovations for people all around the world.

Standing six feet six, Mick has always been attracted to adventure, including motorcycles, snowboarding, surfing, and hang gliding: "If there wasn't a little bit of danger to what I was doing, a little sense of jumping without a net, I didn't see the point," he says.

Taking a leap of faith invigorates Mick. He believes you have to be willing to risk failure in order to succeed.

"Everything begins by taking the part of you that has the false illusion of control and gently pushing it out the window," he says, "so that the other part of you—the part that's willing to take the path that opens up in front of you— can begin to have some fun."

Mick, now forty-six, grew up in Arizona, not rich, but not wanting for anything either. But when the real estate market went south his senior year of high school, his dad's mortgage business all but disappeared. His father tried hard to find a new career, but Mick's mother got two jobs in the meantime. Despite her hectic life, helping others made her happy, so she continued to serve as a volunteer chaplain at a hospital. Mick took notice.

He got his love of helping others from his parents. Both were involved in charities throughout Mick's life. Mick's dad called Mick's mom the "trophy collector" because she won so many awards for her work with charitable causes.

Mick now lives in Venice Beach, California, with his wife and collaborator, Caskey, and their three sons, Angus, Bo, and Trace. Mick calls himself an optimist, a film and TV producer, but first and foremost, a storyteller. Mick makes commercials and trailers, as well as credits sequences and graphics for major movies.

In 2001, Mick and Caskey founded The Ebeling Group (TEG), an award-winning international production company and creative think tank. They had success with commercials and graphics and won several awards for creative design. One of the collectives on Mick's roster, MK12, provided TEG's first big break. Mark Forster, the director of *Stranger Than Fiction*, a film starring Will Ferrell, contacted TEG to do visual effects on the movie. The work garnered positive attention, prompting other directors to seek out TEG. MK12 did the title sequences for *The Kite Runner* and the James Bond film *Quantum of Solace*. It even got a Grammy nomination for the *Quantum of Solace* music video.

Despite these achievements, something still nagged at Mick. A chance encounter while Mick and Caskey were on vacation led the couple to an art exhibit back in Los Angeles. There, they were introduced to the artwork of one of the most well-known graffiti artists in the world.

Tony "Tempt One" Quan was stricken with amyotrophic lateral sclerosis (ALS), known as Lou Gehrig's disease, a degenerative neuromuscular disease that causes full paralysis. Born in 1968 in South Central L.A., a notoriously tough neighborhood associated with gang violence, Tempt majored in art at UC Santa Cruz. While in school, he volunteered at a local recreation center, teaching art to underprivileged kids.

Tempt's unique style and talent led to him painting commissioned graffiti murals. He started the graffiti-art magazine *Big Time*, the first publication to treat graffiti as a serious art form. The art world took notice, and Tempt received requests from galleries all over the world.

But then ALS happened.

Tempt was diagnosed in 2004, and as his disease progressed, he became trapped inside an immovable body, unable to communicate. No longer able to speak to his family, let alone create art, he considered suicide.

When Mick caught wind of Tempt's predicament, he wanted to help in some way, but he didn't know how. He got busy with other projects, but Tempt remained in the back of his mind. After a while, the call to take action was too much.

Mick contacted Tempt's father, and before knowing what he was committing to, Mick promised to find a way for Tempt to communicate with his father. Mick also said Tempt would paint again.

"Say yes first, ask questions later. Commit, then figure it out," Mick says.

Mick had given himself no choice but to come through on his promise. His guiding mantra became: "If I don't do this, who will? And if I don't do it now, then when will I do it?"

The undertaking seemed impossible, but it got Mick wondering if anything is truly impossible. "What if you didn't give yourself the opportunity to fail?" he says. "What if the only limitations on what we do come from our own belief system, our own lack of faith in our ability?"

Caskey took on the project, too, beginning a documentary about Tempt and the graffiti world. She and Mick knew his story would inspire others. Mick "annoyed" enough people until someone agreed to help. "There are times when I am a relentless pit bull and such a pain in the ass that people say 'yes' just to get me the hell out of their office or off the phone," he says.

The Tobii company took an interest in finding a machine to help Tempt. Medicaid finally agreed to fund the machine, called the MyTobii P10, a big computer monitor on a long, adjustable arm. This version had a camera that tracked Tempt's eye movements, so that when he dwelled on a letter, the machine registered the letter and could form words and then sentences. The machine voiced what Tempt registered. Within minutes, Tempt was "talking" on the new device. Thoughts and feelings poured out of him. Tempt's first words in nearly eight years were, "Hey, this is awesome."

But Mick wasn't done. Tempt still needed to create art again. Mick didn't know yet how to make that happen, but he wouldn't stop until he did.

Mick knows the importance of surrounding yourself with the right people. If he can't do something on his own, he finds others who can. So he formed a team of highly intelligent, if eccentric, "crazies" to come up with a remedy.

On Sunday, April 5, 2009, they presented Tempt with his new EyeWriter, an affordable, easily replicable device that would allow Tempt and others with paralysis to communicate and make art using only the movement of their eyes. Being able to draw with his eyes allowed Tempt to be creative again, awakening a joy that had been dormant for years as he lay paralyzed in a hospital bed. Tempt said, "I felt like I had been held underwater, and someone finally reached down and pulled my head up so I could take a breath."

Mick and Caskey made a documentary—*Getting Up: The Tempt One Story*, produced by John Barlow—about Tempt and the creation of the EyeWriter. The film won the 2012 Audience Award at The Slamdance Film Festival, won Best Director at the 2012 Downtown Film Festival Los Angeles, and was an official selection at the Urban World Film Festival, Bend Film Festival, Hawaii International Film Festival, Napa

Valley Film Festival, Other Venice Film Festival, St. Louis International Film Festival, and Reel Abilities Film Festival.

Mick realized he was on the cutting edge of the "Maker" movement, a culture of tech-savvy people who used computers to create amazing inventions. "The people who populated our lives now, the people who were helping me along this wild and crazy path, defined themselves as hackers and 'makers'—which is how I defined myself now, too," he says.

More than three years after the night Mick and Caskey saw Tempt's art, his work was displayed at the Pasadena Museum of California Art. The only question for Mick was what to do next.

His blueprint for success involved three things. First, to have a singular focus; helping one person was the team's initial goal. Second, when you create something of value others can use, give it away. Mick made the EyeWriter open-source, meaning he put the specifications to make the new invention online for any and all to see, free of charge. This would help those in need and would allow others to do their own tinkering to improve the device. Third, his team benefitted from naïveté: "We didn't know that we weren't supposed to be able to do it." Because they didn't consider failure, the team made good on Mick's promise only two and a half weeks after starting the project.

Mick was energized, he says, "because once I had a taste of how far you can go when you make things free and accessible, I was hooked." From that hunger, Mick and Caskey created the Not Impossible Foundation, a nonprofit organization that develops creative DIY technologies to help people overcome difficulties, providing solutions to real-world problems instead of relying on big medical and insurance companies. Their mission was to link and inspire the right people—"crazy lunatic gentlemen and women, to be precise"—to make once seemingly impossible challenges possible.

The project would match people who needed help, like Tempt, with people who could find cheap options for them. The goal: "To just get our hands dirty and take the backs off things, figure out how they work, and jerry-rig something new that could do the job just as well, and then give it away for free." Mick and Caskey invited the whole world to help. They created a website where people could submit their needs and then others could respond with potential resolutions. The motto became, "Help one, help many."

A while later, a friend told Mick about a man named Dr. Tom Catena. Dr. Catena was treating injured people at an isolated hospital in Sudan, northeast Africa, where a vicious civil war raged. Many of the victims were boys who had lost limbs.

Mick immediately thought of Richard Van As, someone he'd recently heard about who was creating prosthetic arms using a 3-D printer. In "a very do-it-yourself crazy hacker way," as Mick describes, Van As could fabricate mechanical "robohands" for amputees. Mick discovered a new cause: "Well, we should just go make hands for them, then."

Mick followed his own advice to take a leap of faith, to commit first and then find a way to make the impossible possible. He figured they could bring 3-D printers to Sudan and work on making arms for boys in need. His friend thought Mick was bluffing, so Mick told him, "Don't challenge me to do something like this. Because if you say let's do it, I'm in."

Mick started researching that night. Thanks to Google, he found what he needed immediately: an article on Dr. Catena in *Time* magazine from April 2012. "Alone and Forgotten, One American Doctor Saves Lives in Sudan's Nuba Mountains" tells the story of Daniel Omar, a boy whose arms were blown off by a bomb dropped by his own government.

Recognizing the sound of an incoming bomb, Daniel had held onto a nearby tree. Doing so spared his life, but his hands were torn off. Daniel was twelve years old.

Daniel ended up in the care of Dr. Catena, who'd stayed behind when his overseers evacuated the treacherous area. The doctor remained to help as many boys as he could, which got Mick to thinking about his own sons, about what he would do if one of them were in Daniel's situation. He thought about his "help one, help many" motto. Knowing he couldn't end the war, Mick at least could help Daniel.

Just like that, "Project Daniel" was under way.

As often happens when someone sets a lofty, noble goal, the stars aligned. Mick contacted Van As, who was willing to help. Mick also reached out to a friend at Intel, and the company agreed to provide computers and money. *National Geographic* got word and wanted to cover the project in an issue on 3-D printing.

Then problems arose. Intel said Project Daniel wouldn't fit into its budget. Mick was to leave for Sudan in less than three weeks and his biggest backer had bailed. He thought about giving up his idea but decided to convince Intel it was making a mistake. "I just came on guns blazing, full force, saying, 'You have to change this,'" Mick explains.

Intel made it happen. Mick would soon be off to find Daniel.

But first Van As, much more familiar with the turmoil in Sudan, sternly cautioned Mick:

> He told us that the moment we hit Sudan soil, we would become targets. That we would be kidnapped by rebels. And that we would witness the most unimaginable of horrors: gutting of pregnant women, hacking off breasts to those with little and newborn babies, execution-style shootings. They line up people and have fun...It is all in the name of terror.

Mick and his team were heading into an atrocious war among tribes and armies. More than two million people had been killed in the region. Hundreds of thousands more had been injured, including fifty thousand amputees. The United Nations has labeled the war one of the worst humanitarian disasters in the world.

Mick could have executive-produced the trip from afar by raising the necessary funds and planning the details before sending a team to get the job done. He had no previous medical or 3-D printer training and knew equally little about the situation in Sudan, where violence could break out at any time, but he felt called to roll up his sleeves. Van As's warning rattled him, "But I also knew that the kid we were focused on was just a kid, just like my kid, and there was no one around to help him, and his whole life depended on someone deciding to take that risk."

A lot of work had to be done in a short amount of time. Mick formed another team of "hackers and makers and general geniuses and crazies" to prepare for the venture. Still worried for his team's safety, he learned from a grizzled wartime documenter: "You wanna save the world? You gotta leave the house."

Not everyone felt the same way. Some of the original team decided against trekking to Sudan. Mick realized he, with no 3-D printer experience, would be the sole maker in the group. Fortunately, Van As told Mick to stop at his home in Johannesburg on his way to find Daniel; Van As would teach Mick how to use the machine.

Dr. Catena was reached via Skype and said he'd found the now-fourteen-year-old Daniel in a sixty-five-thousand-person refugee camp called Yida, which the U.N.

has dubbed "the most challenging refugee camp in the world." Though Mick considered delaying the trip for more preparation time, one of his advisors told him the time was now—conditions in Africa were as good as they were going to be.

Mick was unsure if Daniel would still be in the camp by the time he arrived. In his book, Mick explains his anxiety: "I felt like a mail-order bride being shipped halfway around the world to meet the person I was destined to be with."

He would have less than a week in Johannesburg to learn how to make a mechanical hand with a 3-D printer and some parts from a hardware store. Van As already had figured out how the hand would work, saving Mick valuable time. But Mick wondered if he could produce a working model in a strange land ready to explode further at any minute. Also weighing on his mind were his own three boys, who would spend their first Halloween without him back in Los Angeles.

Knowing creating a hand was far different than fitting a live person with an actual functioning version, Van As had Mick make a device for an amputee named Gideon. The process was laborious, but Mick succeeded:

> That moment set my heart ablaze. The moment
> that someone who you just met, who is missing
> the hand on his left arm, suddenly has one that
> works, fires every synapse in your brain. No drug,
> no sex, no rock and roll, no food, no drink, no

experience—nothing compares to this moment of having created something so simple and yet so profound. Out of nothing, out of a bunch of liquid plastic and a few strings and some cheap bolts from the hardware store, you have given someone a new lease on life.

Still glowing from the experience, Mick learned more about Gideon. What most excited the youth was socializing again. Though he'd been doing okay physically with one hand, emotionally, he'd been struggling. His appearance, being seen as different, embarrassed Gideon. With his new hand, he could be a normal kid again.

Gideon taught Mick a valuable lesson: Often we fight our circumstances, sometimes for a lifetime. But if we learn to accept our fate, we can adapt and overcome just about anything. Helping Gideon—and being helped by him—was just the start.

From Johannesburg, Mick set off for Dr. Catena. Before they met, Mick learned the doctor had operated on more than seven hundred patients, estimating more than eighty percent were civilians. A reporter once asked Dr. Catena why he stayed in the war-torn area, putting his own safety in such peril. Dr. Catena said there was no other option; if he didn't, who would?

Sounds familiar.

Mick called the trip to Sudan "this insane thing we're doing." "It'd be way too overblown to call it our mission, and we're way too disorganized to call it a plan. But we have a distinct goal ahead of us," he said of the journey. Mick's team made it to Juba, a stop on the way to Daniel's camp. Mick was surprised to see people smiling, even laughing, despite the devastation. "It's almost like there's a need to be happy on a molecular level that supersedes your surroundings," Mick observed.

Yet nothing could have prepared the team for what they found when they got to Yida. Mick says, "It was a massive, sprawling, chaotic mess, spread as far as the eye could see." Water, food, clothing, and medical attention were obviously lacking. All types of animals roamed around, and no sanitation system existed. Ramshackle huts made from straw, tarps, and rope sheltered sixty-five thousand people.

"And this was supposed to be a place of refuge," Mick says, sighing. Many refugees had lost everything—most importantly, parents, siblings, spouses, and children. These people were living in a hell.

But Mick noticed something else:

> And yet, once again, I was blown away by the joy I saw. Not by the disgusting nature of the camp, not by the smell, or by the horrendous conditions, or by the thought of how people could possibly live like this, how we as a world can tolerate people living in these conditions.
>
> What blew me away was the joy.

I walked through the camp in kind of a daze, and I saw people laughing and smiling and joking with each other, like it was a perfectly normal day in a perfectly normal town.

The team stayed in a small compound of five tents surrounded by a ten-foot-high fence. They explained their intentions to the overseer of the compound, expressing that they hoped to find Daniel. To their shock, the man motioned, *He is right over there.*

In a nearby hut, Daniel sat with three other amputees. (Daniel's father was off fighting, and Mick was unclear of the whereabouts of his mother.) Daniel wouldn't look at the team, staring forlornly at the dirt. Mick broke the ice with a Mickey Mouse impression, causing Daniel's brother, Shaki, to laugh. Daniel nearly smiled, before averting his gaze again.

Mick learned from the overseer that Daniel had been fitted for prosthetics twice already, but both attempts had been unsuccessful. They weren't functional, and Daniel had taken them off and thrown them on the ground. Daniel had told a reporter previously that he felt useless without hands. His chief concern was making life difficult for his family. "If I could have died," Daniel said, "I would have."

Though they call themselves brothers, Daniel and Shaki are actually distant cousins. "It was kind of amazing to learn of how Shaki had been taking care of Daniel—feeding him, dressing him, wiping him, doing everything for him—without complaint, without fuss, as though it were the most normal thing in the world," Mick says.

Taking Daniel to Dr. Catena's hospital in Gidel was the plan, but a security guard stopped their truck. The ceasefire had ended and the area was now an active war zone. Mick decided the team would get to work the next day right there in the Yida refugee camp and found a larger compound with a kitchen and a tool shed to be their base.

Daniel sat patiently for hours watching Mick work over the next few days. Using his stumps, Daniel made good use of the video games on the tablets the team had brought. Mick recalls, "He was blasting aliens and tossing angry birds around like any suburban kid in America, only doing it in the midst of such primitive surroundings, such bleak devastation."

The excessive heat caused Mick a lot of problems, as the one-hundred-degree temperatures affected the 3-D printers. He chose to print at night in cooler temperatures but quickly found "prehistoric-sized moths," attracted to the printer's light, interrupted the process as much as the heat. Despite these challenges, Mick printed a hand for Daniel after a day.

He now had all the parts necessary, an accomplishment in its own right, but the real challenge would be putting them together and attaching them to a living person…for only the second time in Mick's life. The main objective was to give Daniel a device to enable him to feed himself.

Daniel, disappointed in the past, wasn't sold yet, as Mick shared in his book: "Daniel, in some ways, has the face of an old man; he has a tiredness in his eyes, a world-weary long stare, almost as though he had sunk deep inside himself and saw no good reason to climb back out." Only when Mick made the hand wave at Daniel did the boy break into a huge grin, "the kind that any father of boys knows and loves and lives for; the kind that anyone seeing a skinny, malnourished, dirty, disheveled, beautiful young man who had lost his arms to a senseless, senseless war would take one look at and say, 'I am so lucky to be here, in this moment, to witness this tiny bit of joy amid all this sorrow.'"

The date was November 11, 2013, four months to the day after Mick had decided to undertake this mission.

After modifications to affix the arm, Mick put the hand on Daniel cautiously and . . . it worked! Smacking Shaki playfully upside the head was Daniel's first action with his new hand. Both boys laughed uncontrollably.

A large crowd gathered in the lunch tent as a bowl was put in front of Daniel. The onlookers erupted into laughter, hugs, and cheers when Daniel fed himself for the first time in two years. Someone brought over a brownie, the first chocolate he had ever tasted. Daniel ate three.

Mick, his team, Daniel, and Shaki set off on a ten-hour drive from Yida to see Dr. Catena in Gidel. Mick asked Daniel if they'd be passing the site of the bombing that took his hands. Daniel said they would and agreed to show the way. They ran into Daniel's aunt, who expressed her extreme gratitude to Mick for what he'd given her nephew.

When the group got to Dr. Catena's location, Mick asked Daniel how he felt. Daniel said the accident angered him. After a long pause, he let out a laugh and walked away.

The group met other relatives, neighbors, and friends who hugged Daniel and cried hysterically. Otherwise, Mick found the locals had a cavalier attitude about the war, treating the bombings like they were merely bad weather. For the most part, they went about their lives the best they could.

When it was time to go, Mick put his hand on Daniel's shoulder and, after the boy took one last look back, he felt Daniel's body relax. Something had clicked in him, Mick thought. "Maybe, just maybe, he had decided that it was okay, after all, to be alive," Mick says.

Around midnight, they arrived at the Mother of Mercy Hospital. Dr. Catena gave them a tour of the hospital the next morning. There were two hundred beds, but nearly twice as many patients.

Dr. Catena selected a collection of young men to be trained on the 3-D printer so many more amputees could get a new lease on life, as Daniel now had. Due to the cease-fire, Mick and his team had five days to teach the men how to make arms, instead of the initial plan of fourteen days. Some of these people had never seen a computer.

Gradually, after numerous problems and blunders, they got the hang of the process, managing to make a better "robohand" for Daniel than the one Mick had made in Yida. Dr. Catena entered the room and Mick told Daniel to pick up and toss an Ace bandage to the doctor. Daniel slowly picked up the bandage and rifled "a perfect bullet pass" to the doctor's chest. The cheers in the room were deafening.

Daniel's village had the tools and knowledge to create prosthetics themselves, long after Mick and his team departed. Mick had set out to help one boy—*help one*—and now countless amputees could be fitted with new hands—*help many*.

When they said their goodbyes, Daniel hugged Mick like Mick had never been hugged before. Mick was reluctant to leave, wondering if he'd ever see Daniel and Shaki again. On the plane to Juba, all of the emotions Mick had been holding inside poured out.

But the tears weren't because of the horrors he'd seen, but rather...

...By the feeling of positivity at all I had experienced. The sense of believing in the human spirit, believing in the capability of people to change, believing in their intelligence, in their ability to persevere in spite of all the challenges.

I believe in technology. I believe that technology for the good of humanity can be attained and that people can learn to use anything if there is some inherent good imbedded in it. I believe that anybody given the incentive to do good for the world will most likely strive for that.

I felt proud that I had changed a few people's lives. But I was honored and privileged to think of how much they had changed mine. Because I knew that when I got back to America, nothing was ever going to be the same…

It was not about learning just to appreciate what we have. It was about learning to appreciate all that we are capable of doing.

Mick got home just before Thanksgiving in 2013. Things in Sudan got much worse almost as soon as he left. Thousands were killed in just a few days, including beheadings and the murders of babies. Across the world in Venice Beach, Mick had nightmares many nights. In a sense, he suffered from post-traumatic stress disorder, looking at everything in a different light.

He got word Daniel was alive, but nothing more. Dr. Catena sent him updates every few weeks. In between messages, Mick prayed the boys were safe.

A saving grace for Mick was that people all over the world could make amazing things from the work he'd done and the knowledge he'd shared. Because the Internet has made the world a smaller place, intelligent, creative, and philanthropic individuals and companies are easily connected, able to exchange ideas and work together toward common goals. Thousands of inventions have resulted from the open-source method.

Mick wakes up every morning ecstatic about the work he does and the lives being changed. More and more, the impossible is becoming possible. Limits are being shattered all the time.

Mick and his colleagues are working on all sorts of exciting projects, too numerous to discuss here. His foundation asks people to write in with their own unsolvable medical problems. His band of hackers, artists, designers, and "crazies of all stripes" tries to solve them.

Mick explains, "The beauty of the Not Impossible concept is that we don't actually have to motivate people; we just put the problem out there and wait for motivated people to find us."

This whole journey began for Mick when he and his wife heard about a graffiti artist paralyzed by ALS who was unable to communicate with his family. Two years after inventing the EyeWriter, Mick was contacted by Samsung, one of the biggest technology companies in the world, which said it had modified the device to help many people affected by ALS in South Korea. "I got a huge thrill, a wave of excitement and happiness, when I got that email," Mick says. "It's a perfect example of what can happen when you open-source your world."

Samsung made its model open-source as well, providing software and instructions that would enable anyone to build their own for about $50. The South Korean government agreed to distribute the contraption to more than two hundred patients that year alone.

Unfortunately, as expected, Tempt's ALS has continued to progress. Mick says his friend loses control of his eye movements, so using the ocular-recognition technology is challenging. Mick's team is working on a new version of the machine using brain waves instead. "But even with all that," Mick says, "Tempt remains his usual positive, funny self."

In January 2015, Mick released *Not Impossible: The Art and Joy of Doing What Couldn't Be Done.* He returned to Sudan in November 2016 to test his latest prosthetic project, "Prosthetic in a Box." He not only saw Daniel but got Daniel and Shaki out of Sudan and into school in Nairobi, Kenya. "[Daniel] is everything you would expect a teenage boy to be," Mick quips. "Funny, awkward, curious, and hungry!"

Mick has added "speaker" to his list of talents. His TED Talk has more than a million views online, and he has spoken on every continent except Antarctica. "Everything that's possible today was impossible (or seemed impossible) first," Mick says.

Asked recently how he stays focused on one task with so much going on in his life, Mick responds: "I don't. I'm so passionate about the work we are doing, my team is so dedicated, we always have about a dozen irons in the fire. What I do stay focused on is our creating defiant solutions for the world's overlooked and underserved people. With that as the driver, we can tackle hunger, accessible prosthetics, vision health, helping Daniel get an education, building maker labs in refugee camps, celebrating other groups who are doing amazing work—the list goes on."

*Help one, help many.*

*If I don't do this, who will? And if I don't do it now, then when will I do it?*

Mick says that if you take away only one thing from his story, let it be that you can do anything you set your mind to. "I promise you, if you take the time to consider it, you'll find ways to amaze yourself," he says. "And maybe, just maybe, find a path to walk that you've never walked before. It may be a kind of maze, there may be a lot of twists and turns—but trust me. It's worth it because of what you find at the end."

..................................................................................

You can find more information about Mick Ebeling at mickebeling.com and notimpossible.com. If you would like to make a donation to the Not Impossible Foundation in honor of Mick Ebeling, please email media@notimpossible-labs.com.

# Sarah

The 2008 recession in the United States both crippled Sarah Greene and served as her call to action. The economic crisis doomed her photography business, so Sarah turned the focus from her own situation to spotlight the plight of others around the country in a photographic journal. At forty-six years old, she set off on a ten-state journey from Sussex County, Delaware, armed with a laptop, notebooks, and a camera.

Sarah talked to and photographed people in shelters and in food lines, as well as homeless living on the streets over four months. She explains: "I went in search of hardships due to the recession. What I discovered was many different circumstances creating crisis in people's lives. Some were the economy, some were self-inflicted, and there were many other real-life situations that changed people's lives for the worse. What I found surprised me."

A professional photographer, Sarah had built her business primarily on wedding photography and portraits. Her work also has appeared in *Artemis*, a book of art and poetry; *The Chronicle of the Horse*; and *The Cape Gazette* in Delaware. She shot a cover photo for *Aussie Times*, a magazine about Australian Shepherds, and she was the still photographer for the 2013 movie *House of Good and Evil*, shot in the next town over from hers.

Sarah dropped out of school at the age of sixteen, saying high school just wasn't right for her. In 1979, at seventeen, she left Washington, D.C., and moved to Southern California. She had sent money ahead of her to a friend of a friend to secure an apartment. When she arrived, Sarah learned that "friend" had blown Sarah's money on drugs.

She ended up broke and homeless in San Diego, forced to eat at missions. Though beds were available for men, there were not enough for women and children. Sarah says, "I slept on the streets for several weeks, in doorways outside, in movie theaters, and on strangers' couches." She is grateful that others reached out to her, and she realizes that many in her situation weren't lucky enough to find helping hands.

Sarah told her father she desperately needed money, but she didn't tell him she was homeless for fear of alarming him. She found work in light construction, saved money, and was able to get an apartment. Sarah earned her GED when she was twenty-two and went to college at twenty-six. At twenty-nine, she graduated with honors and two associate's degrees from San Diego City College; she later graduated from the School of the Art Institute of Chicago with a Bachelor of Fine Arts.

Years later, on April 4, 2004, a faulty extension cord caused a fire that destroyed Sarah's home. Sarah still feels indebted to the Red Cross, which gave her a jacket, a toothbrush, and toothpaste. She also received a gift card to buy clothes, plus three nights' lodging in a motel. "They told me they normally gave more, but donations were way down," Sarah says.

Not immune to struggle in her own life, Sarah felt her life experiences made her more understanding of others barely keeping their heads above water. "I've had great misfortunes in my own life," she acknowledges. "I believe those experiences have made me more empathetic to the miseries of those I meet."

When the recession hit her business, Sarah sold her car and purchased a minivan, which would serve as her home and office on the road. She believed that capturing photographs of the people she would meet would have a strong impact on anyone who saw her work, which she plans to self-publish in the book *Too Hungry to be Proud: A Photographic Journal of 'One Thing' That Changed Their Lives.*

"The purpose of my project is to focus awareness of the growing poverty and homelessness in America through the visual power of photography...driving and recording our neighbors there who are enduring the hardships of everyday life without adequate food or shelter," Sarah explains. "As the numbers of these families are growing across the country, it is important that this problem be illustrated."

Before Sarah left, her mother, Zina Greene, who had long contributed to organizations working to end homelessness, paid for Sarah to attend an Association of Community Organizations for Reform Now (ACORN) convention in Detroit. Sarah learned how ACORN educated those in need and helped save people's homes.

She shared her project idea with some ACORN leaders, who graciously pointed her to subjects she could interview along the way. For example, the New Orleans affiliate collected money to help with Sarah's travel expenses. (ACORN was at one time the nation's largest organization working for social justice and stronger communities.)

With a cooler and a sleeping bag in her minivan, Sarah set off to travel the United States. Figuring conditions would be harshest in the middle of the summer, Sarah headed south from Delaware on July 12, 2008. In addition to those to whom ACORN led her, Sarah says, "I found people through food banks, missions, on the street, through people I met, churches—anywhere I could find people willing to share their stories and allow me to capture their image. I then let the road take me where it would for the rest of my journey."

Sarah found statistics highlighting the plight of the United States in 2008:

• According to *The New York Times*, 2.6 million jobs were lost, the worst year since 1945.

• According to CNN Money, U.S. foreclosure filings spiked by more than 81 percent. More than 3.1 million foreclosures were issued.

• According to The Alliance Report, the number of homeless people increased three percent, or by about twenty thousand people. The number of homeless families increased four percent.

Many of the downtrodden Sarah met struggled with addictions, came from broken homes, or had deceased parents.

Others had histories of being abused. Sarah tried to capture it all. "When I witnessed emotion or saw just the right shot, I lowered my pen and raised my camera," she says.

At times, Sarah's expectations were upended, and much of what she found shocked her. Many of those who had fallen on tough times had college degrees. Many were disabled; many were veterans. "It was surprising to me how many looked like they did not belong there," Sarah says, sighing. "Many looked the same as my friends and neighbors." She realized many Americans are only one or two steps from being in the same spot as the people she met on her journey.

Sarah met people who lived in parks and in the woods. Some slept in sleeping bags right on the street. One couple walked five miles a day applying for jobs, but they hadn't found any openings. Often, previous convictions kept people from gaining employment. Others were still devastated by Hurricane Katrina, which had uprooted their once-stable lives. Many were in a holding pattern, on assistance waiting lists for a year, even two. For example, an organization in Waco, Texas, which previously served one hundred clients a month, was then overloaded with one hundred *a day*.

In her photographic documentary, Sarah tells the story of Courtney, age twenty-seven, in North Carolina. Doing her best to raise three kids, Courtney needed to go into fast-food restaurants so her children could use the bathroom. Staff would not permit them to do so, saying only customers had bathroom privileges. Courtney was humiliated.

Dealing with pride and low self-esteem was a common theme. In fact, Sarah said approaching people with respect and dignity was one of her biggest concerns. One elderly woman told her, "I was too proud to go [to an agency] for help until...I was too hungry to be proud."

After going home for a few months to collect more money (not only did her mother's friends and Sarah's friends and family donate money for her project, but people she met along the road donated as well), Sarah began Phase II of her photographic documentary in November 2008. The additional funds would pay for gas and occasional hotel stays for a shower and a decent night's sleep. This time, Sarah chose to head north through New England in the unforgiving winter months. She found more of the same desolation, often a direct result of the national economic upheaval.

Sarah talked to one couple at their wits' end. Their son had severe health problems, so the mother left her job to stay home as a caretaker. Her husband, a Boston College graduate, had been the senior vice president at a bank. When the bank was bought out, he lost his job. They eventually lost their house and moved into an apartment. When Sarah met them, they were worried they would lose that in a short amount of time, too, while the man looked for a new career. His wife said she'd wake up some days in disbelief that this was now their life.

Sarah faced challenges of her own on her trips. During the extreme summer heat, the food in her cooler sometimes spoiled. Shower access was scarce. Gas cost more than $4 a gallon.

Finding a place to park her van for the night was a frequent hassle, especially if she couldn't find a proper rest stop.

One cold night in Massachusetts, a banging noise startled Sarah awake. A police officer was knocking snow off her van to check her license plate. When she opened the van door, terrified and in her long johns, four police cars had their lights shining on Sarah. Though she explained her purpose—she was living like the homeless, but not homeless herself—the officers gruffly told her she was parked on private property and ordered her to leave the state. She couldn't control her shaking as she quickly left for New Jersey. Sarah still regrets missing an interview scheduled for that next morning, having no way to contact the individual to say she would miss their appointment.

But not everything she found was gloom and doom. In her book, Sarah describes finding hope, courage, and resilience. She found many individuals trying to kick long-term addictions, doing all they could to secure employment. Several times she met people who had been successful obtaining housing and employment and then dedicated their lives to helping others in positions they had been in not long before. After all, they knew the challenges and wanted to assist any way they could. Still others found a saving grace, saying religion was the only thing that kept them alive.

The kindness of small-business owners, so many of whom generously donated to food banks and missions, was overwhelming, Sarah says. Finding people in horrible circumstances still so positive, so hopeful, continuously surprised her. "The spirit of people is really powerful," she points out. Sarah frequently found that people looked much happier than she had expected.

She returned home on Christmas Eve 2008. When she looks back on the adventure today, she doesn't know how she pulled it off: "How did I do that?" she wonders. Sarah's road-trip project left her with fond memories, even among all the despair. She also gained a new appreciation for what she does have. She says:

> [The] most difficult thing overall is realizing how much I *do* have as I see more and more people with less. I find myself looking at people all the time wondering if they know or care about the losses of others. I am amazed at how many people are devoted at the food pantries I have been to day after day, year after year, as volunteers.
>
> I realized my circumstances were not nearly as dire as I thought they were. All the people I met and interviewed touched my heart. I worry about many of them, where they are now. Did they save their homes, find homes, or find solutions to their individual dire situations?
>
> I had my own struggles on the road: finding safe places to park and sleep, sleeping in a van, lack of showers, food going bad, gaining people's trust to open up to me with their stories, and raising money

for my project. But I had the most wonderful experiences with the people I met, interviewed, and photographed. I built bonds with some of them. I had great experiences in every state…I truly wanted to cover the entire United States, but life doesn't always work out as you plan it. I am blessed that so many people trusted in me. I was able to utilize my passion of photography to capture them, as well as share their stories of sadness and hope.

I know there are so many more stories to be told. I was inspired by the many people who manage to live through such heartbreaking hardships with courage, faith, and strength of character.

Sarah, now fifty-five, lives in Floyd County, Virginia, with her two rescue kitties and toy Australian Shepherd. She enjoys her rural living, about an hour from the nearest superstore. She credits her mom and dad for giving her a heart for helping others. "Both of my parents gave of themselves," she recalls. "That is how I was raised."

Sarah volunteers at Plenty!, a grassroots food bank and farm in Floyd County, Virginia, and distributes vegetables to needy families lacking transportation. She is also passionate about her involvement as an elected board member of New River Community Action (NRCA), a federally funded nonprofit organization that works with community groups to address poverty. NRCA teaches good parenting and budgeting skills, helps people get GEDs, and brings books to children. Its programs include emergency financial assistance; a "Head Start" program involving the entire family in education, social services, medical care, and nutrition for children under the age of five; rent, housing, and mortgage help; assistance for ex-offenders transitioning back into the community; and education and counseling for acquiring housing, among other programs.

Sarah still takes photos, but mostly for herself these days. Still amazed that the people she met were so grateful to share their stories, Sarah feels they were the ones helping her. Because of her own obstacles, she understood her subjects on a deep level, believing, "We are all just two paychecks away from homelessness." Sarah's pictures, both uplifting and heartbreaking, show the faces behind the stories, taking the message to a deeper level.

Sarah points out that many resources are available if people know where to look, and she says many devoted people are making a difference in a great number of lives. "Isn't it funny how the people that give are so thankful?" she asks. "It's just heartwarming."

She asks that you consider donating food, clothing, or money if you can, wherever you feel it's most needed. "Remember, it only takes one thing to alter your life. Sometimes it can be devastating," she says from experience. "Be kind, especially to those who have had one thing throw them into a bad situation."

........................................................................

If you would like to make a donation in honor of Sarah Greene, please do so at Feeding America (feedingamerica. org).

# Phillip

Phillip A. Singleton never thought he'd be involved with politics. He wanted to be a cook, learning by his grandmother's side as a child, and his dream was to open a restaurant in Philadelphia.

A first-generation American of Jamaican descent, Phillip was raised in South Florida with a younger sibling. "We weren't poor," he says. "We were between middle class and poor."

When Phillip was thirteen, his mom told him he needed to help support his family. He took a job bagging groceries, an experience that helped him "know what it's like to earn money." His strong work ethic led him to jobs at Pizza Hut, a Marriott hotel, and Dillard's department store.

Phillip, who had run his high school newspaper, earned a journalism scholarship to Florida A&M University in 2003. Most weekdays he went to school from 7 a.m. to 1 p.m. and then worked at a DoubleTree Hotel from 3 p.m. to 11 p.m.

Despite his drive, two weeks before his semester finals in November 2008, Phillip found himself unemployed when the DoubleTree downsized. In need of money, Phillip left school. For a period of time, he was homeless, living out of his car or sleeping on friends' floors.

His lifelong love for hip-hop music inspired Phillip during this tough time, specifically "Street Lights" by Kanye West. "I don't know why that song resonated with my soul, but my intuition told me that despite the downfall, I was on the verge of something that would change my life forever," Phillip explains.

His break came in the form of a newly elected official whose many stays at the DoubleTree had let him witness Phillip's hard work firsthand. Phillip asked if the official needed a staff member, and though the man already had a candidate in mind, he gave Phillip a chance. Phillip says, "I stepped out on faith and took an unpaid internship in the Florida House of Representatives working for Representative Dwayne Taylor and the Democratic Minority Office.

"I briefly went back to college in 2009 and [am] still in the process of completing my degree...I decided to start my career in politics because I was getting real-life experience and there were not a lot of other opportunities out there at the time. Unfortunately, working around the clock in Florida's political process—from running campaigns to passing laws and working with elected officials—delayed my progress in completing my degree, but it's something I have focused on completing since."

This drastic move changed the course of Phillip's life in a profound way. He quickly found he had a passion for politics, well-served by his "Rain Man-like memory." He felt called to help underrepresented groups, such as minorities, in government issues. "Little did I know that my years of customer service experience…would put me in a position to get a full grasp of the policies and politics that impact the everyday people I serve," Phillip says.

The internship helped Phillip secure a job as a research assistant at Pittman Law Group. "I worked there for five years, working my way up from that role into the legislative director's position where I handled lobbying, political campaigns, and advocacy work for clientele throughout the entire state," he says.

By 2010, at the age of twenty-four, Phillip had become the youngest African-American lobbyist in Florida's history. He helped pass legislation to expand Major League Soccer in Florida, helped further the Break Pay Scholarship for post-9/11 G.I. Bill student veterans, and has secured millions of dollars in state funding for various economic-development projects. Phillip's influence in the Florida legislature got him recognized as "an Emerging Leader in Politics" in 2011 by the Florida Conference of Black State Legislators. *850 Business Magazine* also tabbed Phillip as a "Top 40 under 40," and the Network of Young Professionals named him one of its "Top 20 Under 40 Emerging Leaders."

In September 2014, Phillip founded his own full-service governmental affairs and multicultural outreach firm, Singleton Consulting. He has worked with Fortune 500 companies, the Florida legislature, collegiate sports teams, and the banking industry.

Singleton Consulting lobbies important issues to elected officials, gives political and legislative guidance to those unsure of where to start, and helps groups and individuals develop brands and implement campaigns. His website clarifies: "We fall in love with your problems...then deliver your solution."

"We understand the policies, the process of how a bill becomes law, and how to influence our client's interest before it's too late," Phillip says. "We have built relationships on both sides of the aisle and can put you in front of the decision-makers you need to reach on the issues that are important to your future."

Phillip is now thirty-one years old. Due to his love of music and politics, he branded himself with a clever moniker: the Hip Hop Lobbyist.

Phillip created this persona because of his love of the musical genre and as a way to relate to underrepresented people and groups. Because politics involves a lot of egos and emotion, Phillip says he uses music to keep him centered and grounded.

His company helps minority organizations that are not getting proper representation. "Our clients benefit from having a trusted ally working behind closed doors who can strategically advance or derail issues that could impact their future," Phillip says.

A typical day for Phillip ends at 1 a.m. He wakes up by 5 or 6 a.m. to check e-mail, watch the news, and then meet with elected officials. Phillip says Florida has a sixty-day legislative session, so you must be strategic in a short time: "It is a mental chess game."

Part of Phillip's strategy involves . . . his socks. The more outlandish, the better. After all, Phillip points out, politics is about building relationships. "The socks become something to talk about," he says.

Phillip, a Democrat, knows how to talk to people on both sides of the aisle. And typically, those people do not look much like him. Phillips says that out of 1,800 or so lobbyists in Florida, only thirty are minorities.

Though many people he encounters are attorneys, Phillip doesn't see the need to become a lawyer to thrive. Armed with an excellent memory and "a diehard commitment to work for everything," which his mom taught him at a young age, Phillip is confident he holds his own with seasoned lawyers.

Phillip overcame being unemployed and homeless by staying focused and putting forth sustained maximum effort. He has come a long way, but he hasn't abandoned his first love: the passion for cooking he developed alongside his grandmother.

Phillip says: "Outside of politics, running political campaigns, cooking, and teaching more people about the cultural diversity of Millennials—the future of our nation—I'm just an everyday guy trying to become the first lobbyist to ever win a Grammy award."

If anyone can do it, it's Phillip A. Singleton.

...........................................................................

You can learn more about Phillip A. Singleton at phillipsingleton.com or connect with him on Twitter @HipHopLobbyist. If you would like to make a donation in honor of Phillip, please do so at Boys & Girls Clubs of America (bgca.org).

# Laurie

Many people who grow up to be lights for others were affected positively by one or both of their parents. This is not one of those stories.

In her book *Finding My Own Voice: A Story of Abuse, Addiction, and Freedom*, Dr. Laurie Turner shares her traumatic personal story to raise awareness about child abuse and addiction. At one point in her life, Laurie questioned why she was even born and why she should continue living. Today, Laurie has turned things around. "For the first time in my life, I feel at peace," she says. "I'm comfortable in my own skin."

It took a long and bumpy road for her to get there. "By the grace of God, I am not dead or in prison," Laurie says. "For some reason, I have been spared. God must have a plan for me. I don't know what the plan is, except that I know that sobriety is part of the plan."

Laurie was raised in Bell Gardens, a suburb of Los Angeles. The main things she remembers from her childhood are her mom's constant fear, deep sadness, and habitual crying.

"I do not think the abuse started until after she married Dad," Laurie says of her mother. "He would scare and yell at her often. He called her names like 'Nazi lover' because she was German."

Physical beatings left bruises on Laurie's mom's body, and nothing Laurie's mom did made her husband happy.

Laurie's dad was a "bad-ass man," connected to the Hells Angels motorcycle club. Drugs were common in the house. Once, Laurie's mom answered a knock on the door, and a man fell dead across the threshold. Laurie's father made a phone call to friends who took away the body.

One of Laurie's earliest memories of her father is from when Laurie was four or five. Her father held her mother by the throat, threatening to hunt her down and kill her if she ever left him. On her dad's angriest drunken nights, Laurie and her mom would take refuge in the homes of family and friends, but they always went back in the morning.

The tension was so intolerable that Laurie tried to kill herself when she was around six years old. Her parents were fighting, as usual; her dad was drinking, and her mom was crying once again. Laurie went into the kitchen, climbed up onto the countertop, and swallowed every pain reliever and pill she found in the cabinets. She lay down on the couch and woke up in the hospital, where her stomach was pumped. Her mom yelled at her in the car on the way home. All Laurie knew was she was headed back to her prison.

Laurie writes in her book:

> With drugs, alcohol, and domestic abuse, there was chaos. My home life was everything outside of *normal*. My mom worked all day, sometimes working two jobs to feed my father's habits and to

keep a roof over our heads. I remember spending most of my time with him. Mom usually wasn't around much. I cannot remember her too well.

Laurie's mother had had a tough past but kept her issues bottled up. She was born to alcoholic parents and had to grow up too soon, basically raising herself and her brother as a young girl. Laurie's father was born in Kentucky and had had an even worse upbringing. His mother was raped by an angry, drunken sailor on leave during World War II when she was sixteen. Laurie's grandmother reported the rape to her own mom and older sister, who ordered her to marry her attacker. She relented, and the couple had two children together.

Laurie says her grandmother "hated her life—forced to marry someone she loathed, forced to have his children, forced to live a life in which she didn't have a say." Laurie's grandmother was very talented and left her children to pursue a theater career in Hollywood. Because Laurie's grandfather was mostly at sea in a submarine, Laurie's father and his sister stayed with their grandparents.

The grandparents were prone to drinking moonshine and fighting, and they physically abused their grandchildren. Laurie's grandmother returned to her kids after five years, but the damage was already beyond repair. To make matters worse, Laurie's grandmother also abused her kids after her homecoming. "The cycle of violence goes back at least four generations on my father's side of the family," Laurie says.

In high school, Laurie's father fell in love with a Hispanic girl. When he proclaimed his feelings for her, she didn't return the sentiment, saying her father would forbid her to date a white man, especially one with a reputation for being a womanizer. Laurie's father ran to a nearby downed power line, saying he'd electrocute himself if the girl wouldn't have him. He made good on his threat.

The shock threw Laurie's father a hundred yards. A life squad rushed him to a burn unit, where he stayed for nine months. Due to gangrene, he lost his left arm from the elbow down. A star baseball player hoping to play college and professional baseball, her father saw his life take a one-hundred-eighty-degree turn. He lost his arm, his scholarship hopes, and his future.

In her book, Laurie recalls:

> All his dreams died, and he died with them. He was mentally washed up before life even began for him. The only thing left to do was to feel sorry for himself, blame others for his situation, get drunk, and use a lot of drugs. Trust me: He did it well.

Laurie's mother worked nights for a phone company, and her dad often came home drunk, keeping Laurie up late into the night by furiously retelling his childhood. Laurie came to see her great-grandparents and grandmother as monsters. "Those people should have been locked away without a key," she says.

Her father's drunken rants transformed into something much more sinister.

"I am not sure how old I was when my father first started abusing me, and I can't remember what abuse started first: sexual, physical, emotional, or verbal," Laurie says. "But based on my years in therapy, I would say sexual, followed by physical and verbal abuse."

Laurie yearned for the love and acceptance she saw in other families, "but instead I experienced yelling, pure hatred, pushing, punching, glaring, strangling, name-calling, uninvited sexual encounters, slapping, emotional starvation, and belittling," she says. To get by, she created a private self and a public self, the latter essential to surviving her childhood. "My public self didn't take any shit from anyone," she says.

Laurie writes:

> I worked very hard at isolating myself, not allowing others to get too close to me. I only showed others what I needed them to see. I am always in *control…* a master at hiding my feelings and emotions. I had to sacrifice my true identity, changing who I was in order to please others. In time, I became an actor portraying myself. My true identity never fully emerged throughout my childhood; I feared people would run from me.

Laurie's parents met when her mother was twenty and her father was twenty-five. Laurie's mother soon got pregnant, and the two married out of obligation. Her mother left college to work, while her father partied. Laurie believes her mother saw her as an inconvenience, blaming her unhappy life on Laurie. Laurie doesn't recall any positive childhood memories.

Laurie learned in later years that her aunt and grandmother had suspected that Laurie's father was molesting Laurie. They both filed paperwork in Orange County, California, to gain custody of Laurie, but nothing happened, because Laurie's father moved the family from California to Washington.

Laurie's mother continued working at a telephone company to support the family, while her dad drank. The physical abuse escalated, and her father began threatening his wife and daughter with knives.

Repeatedly, Laurie pleaded with her mom to leave him. Laurie fantasized about them packing their bags while he was away and driving off into the sunset. But her mom just shook her head and cried. Laurie knew then her mother would never leave her father, no matter what he did. "She would just succumb to the verbal abuse, continue to cover up the bruises, and tuck down the emotional despair," Laurie says, sighing.

A lone comfort for Laurie was her first true friend, a blond Labrador retriever who lived a few houses away. She felt a special connection to him and told the dog everything. For Laurie, it was her first real experience of love.

Laurie spent many nights home alone, going without dinner. But one night, her father beat her so badly that she couldn't sit down at school the next day. Laurie's teacher noticed, and authorities were called. Laurie, a second-grader, was sent to a foster home.

She recalls:

> I'll tell you up front that I did not like foster care at all and I made a promise not to go back. I couldn't comprehend at that time what I needed in terms of emotional or verbal support, but I knew that I didn't want to be beaten by my father anymore. I don't think anyone can understand what I felt. I didn't. Put yourself in a child's position. Any child who cries out for help is taking a risk, an unforeseeable risk. Picture yourself building up enough self-esteem to tell someone who you trust, such as a teacher, family member, or friend, that you were beaten by a parent, a person who was supposed to love you and care for you. Then at that moment of vulnerability, you are ripped away from everything you know to be placed in another world, a world in which you don't recognize nor know the rules.

A social worker told Laurie her father had been arrested and sentenced to attend an alcohol treatment center with a focus on anger management. After her dad completed the treatment, Laurie went home. As soon as his probation period ended, Laurie's dad moved the family. Laurie was eight.

She began sleeping in a closet as her safe place. She would fantasize about running away and even dreamed of killing her parents. Laurie got in trouble at school, seeking attention and talking back to teachers. She struggled with her classes, especially math. (Laurie mixed up the orders of numbers, learning as an adult that she is dyslexic, a trait common to her family.)

She wanted to fit in, but felt like the weird kid. Laurie didn't have the social skills to make friends. Classmates picked on her. After school, Laurie would sit in front of the TV at home, nervously awaiting the sound of her father's truck pulling up to the house. She felt ugly, alone, and powerless.

One night, her father came home bloody after an apparent fight. He punched a hole in the wall near Laurie's head, screaming at her to tell the police he'd been home all night if they came looking.

Laurie felt exhausted and helpless. "That was the last straw," she says. "Something broke inside of me that night."

She writes in her book:

> This was it. Courage. I was so tired of surviving. I was tired of being afraid. I was tired of being angry, bitter, crushed, and betrayed by my father and mother. I no longer had the energy to separate the truth from lies. I was tired of being threatened and getting beat up by Dad or, worse, listening to my mother belittling me and experiencing her vindictive behaviors. Remember: Bruises go away, but

words may stay with you for a lifetime to replay over and over again in your head.

The next night, Laurie waited for her father to come home. She knew he'd be drunk and might take his anger out on her once again. But she'd had enough.

Laurie picked up a loaded shotgun, crept down the steps, turned the corner to face her father, and raised the weapon. "I started crying, tears running down my face, and said, 'You will never hurt me again,' and pulled the trigger," she says.

The shotgun's safety was locked, and the gun did not fire. Laurie's dad didn't do or say anything. He walked past Laurie, went upstairs to pack a suitcase, and left.

Laurie believes her story begins here.

The best year of her young life was 1986. After her sophomore year of high school, at age fifteen, Laurie spent the summer with her father's mom, happy to be in a new location. "At the time, my grandmother and her husband, Tom, were Baptist missionaries and lived in a border town called Agua Prieta, Mexico," she recalls. "I was fortunate to spend the summer working with the Mexican children, telling Bible stories, feeding the poor, and handing out Christian tracts."

The Mexican children were very accepting of Laurie, and she played volleyball with them every night. They went on walks together. She felt free, accepted, and safe. For the first time in her life, Laurie had hope.

At the summer's end, with her father out of the picture, Laurie and her mom moved again, this time to a suburb outside Vancouver, Washington. Laurie liked the change, seeing this as an opportunity to start over. No one knew her there or knew of her painful history.

Laurie's mother suffered periodic breakdowns, staying in her room for hours or even days, depressed. Ashamed and alone, Laurie gave in to peer pressure and began using drugs and drinking beer, wine, and liquor at the age of sixteen—despite hating alcohol for ruining her family. "I didn't realize until it was almost too late that I was destroying myself for actions that I was forced to partake in as a child," she says.

She smoked marijuana and hung out with the party crowd. Laurie felt relaxed and less awkward socially when high. Substances helped her cope with her life and eased her painful memories. She made a lot of friends and thought her new life had healed her difficult past. Laurie skipped school to smoke pot and dated druggies, drunks, and fighters—men much like her father.

Laurie soon got into cocaine, crack, speed, crystal meth, and acid and barely graduated from high school. "I would guzzle beer before school, sitting in the school's parking lot," she says. "Then, I would snort coke in the school's bathrooms during passing period."

After taking some additional remedial math and English classes, Laurie went to Mount Hood Community College for the fall semester, driving forty-five minutes one way to attend. Laurie liked the school, but she made some new party friends and flunked out in the first semester.

Laurie went to Clark Community College the following winter. She did well and signed up for classes at Mount Hood again, but then she got mononucleosis and was sick for two months. She had to drop all of her classes.

While recovering, Laurie got the idea to attend a college far away, one where she wouldn't be tempted to party. Her search led her to Liberty University, a Christian college in Lynchburg, Virginia. Using loans and grant money, she flew off for a new adventure in 1990, removed from her wild friends.

But her hopes were short-lived, as she writes in her book:

> I have to say that I have moved so many times, hoping to reinvent myself, but I always brought my true self along with every move. I started college with high hopes. I even became a Christian girl. I accepted Jesus in my heart but found it difficult to change my behavior and actions with alcohol always around.

Her stay at Liberty was brief. Kicked out of school, Laurie was essentially homeless, and she continued down self-destructive paths. A few of her drug-dealing friends were shot, other friends tried to commit suicide while on meth, and some went to prison. The anger she'd buried inside reared its head as violence. She picked fights with females and males alike, always trying to prove herself.

Laurie says she was not stupid, but she concedes to having been highly dysfunctional. Her past drug use affects her even today. "I cannot remember things and am slow to process information," she says. "I have to turn information over in my head and think about it for a while; then, sooner or later, an answer comes, but by then it might be too late."

At the age of twenty-three, then living in Nevada, Laurie was drinking every day, and the drug problems of those around her had gotten old and dangerous. She quit using drugs and decided to get away from the unhealthy scene. She moved back to Vancouver.

About seven months later, in January 1993, she reconnected with a friend's older brother—and was pregnant two months later. Laurie moved in with her baby's father but soon learned he was drinking, using drugs, and sleeping with other women. Eight months pregnant, she left.

Laurie attracted the same type of guy over and over, she writes:

> I wasn't good at relationships. I didn't communicate well, and fighting became the norm. I didn't learn how to solve problems, compromise, and love unconditionally. I was always on guard, lacking any stability and trust.

Laurie's son, Steven, was born a week before Christmas. Laurie would raise him on her own with her mom's help. Realizing she had to get her life in order, Laurie quit smoking, worked part-time, and went back to college full-time, now as a serious student. She was determined to limit her drinking to a few glasses of wine on occasion. Laurie says, "I was going to be a mom, and dammit, I was going to be a good mom."

Laurie tried to curtail her drinking, but she always found an excuse to break her own rules. She rarely ate actual food, drinking instead. "Somehow I crossed that imaginary line in which I had stopped drinking for fun and started drinking for need," Laurie says. "I just know that I spent my time either planning my next drink or trying to control my environment as I drank."

She drove drunk many times, even with Steven in the car, which she is ashamed of now. She got two DUIs. Laurie knew she had a problem, but she wasn't sure what to do or where to turn. Laurie lost the trust of her friends, and her shame would not let her look at her reflection in the mirror. "By the time my drinking career was over," she says, "I was drinking daily with reoccurring nervous breakdowns for which anti-depressant medication was no longer working."

But then, Laurie had an epiphany:

> I realized how lucky I really was. I had made so many bad decisions, put myself in situations that could have led me to jail, prison, or death. I had been drinking and using for half my life. The secrets I had kept! The relationships I had destroyed! The lying, running, stealing, and surviving lifestyle had taken its toll on me.

Looking for relief, Laurie read books about adult children of alcoholics. She could relate to the stories, which were much like her own, but didn't find any solutions. She had gone to one Alcoholics Anonymous meeting when she was nineteen, but she felt no connection to the people and never returned.

Then one day, she met Pam. Pam was a new waitress at the restaurant where Laurie worked, a single mother very open about being a recovering alcoholic. The two became friends, and Laurie began asking her about sobriety.

Laurie poured her heart out in their conversations, revealing things she had bottled up her whole life. Pam listened patiently, without judgment. Laurie trusted Pam—the first time she had trusted anyone.

Laurie hit bottom when she found out her boyfriend was cheating with a friend of hers. She broke every plate she owned and drank all the alcohol in her home. Unsure what to do, Laurie called Pam.

Pam told her to get on her knees and pray. Laurie did as told and asked God for help. Pam came over the next morning to help clean up the broken glass and Laurie's shattered soul. Pam said it was time Laurie learned about AA.

Pam took Laurie, then thirty, to an AA meeting on July 14, 2000. After the AA meeting with Pam, Laurie returned home to think. She was scared but also excited. Laurie felt a calming peace, a confidence that everything would be okay.

She couldn't go to a treatment facility because she had to care for her son, so Laurie chose to quit drinking cold turkey. She went to a lot of AA meetings, but sobriety wasn't easy. She recalls:

The first ninety days were physically torture. Without alcohol in my system, my body started to go through withdrawals: pain, tremors, and shakes are what I remember. It is hard to describe. My body ached. I had physical pain. Every nerve in my body was on fire. I was burning up. I was feverish. I sweated out the booze. I still can smell the stench. I stunk. My head and stomach ached. I couldn't eat. I just lay in bed, couldn't even stand up—had to crawl to the bathroom. I would sit in the shower and let hot water pour over my body.

The shakes were the worst. I couldn't stop my hands from shaking. I had to sit on them to keep them from moving. I was lucky in that my new job understood. It turned out that my new boss was also a recovering alcoholic and saw the signs. I still had to bartend to keep me from worrying about money. Sometimes making and carrying drinks was difficult. In many cases, I had to remake the drinks because I spilled half of them. I looked like death even with a pound of makeup on. I worked the minimum hours needed to pay my rent and bills. I slept all morning, rolling out of bed just in time to go to a noon meeting, then got ready for work, worked my shift, came home, and stayed up half the night because I couldn't fall asleep. Then I did it all over again, day after day...

…I used to drink away feelings; now I had to deal with them head-on. Sometimes it was unbearable. I often cried out, blaming myself or others, especially my mom and dad, for all my misfortunes. Guilt weighed heavily on my heart, as well as fear, anger, loneliness, and pain.

Six-year-old Steven saw what was going on and worried about his mom. "Kids aren't stupid," Laurie says. "He knew something was wrong."

To her credit, she was honest with her son, admitting she had to stop drinking and that her "special meetings" were to help her do so. Laurie gradually gained strength. She wrote her feelings on paper, worked in her yard in the sunshine, painted her living room, cooked, worked on puzzles with Steven—any project to keep her busy. She also found out who her true friends were.

Pam was front and center, Laurie says:

Pam came over to help me during those early months of sobriety. She was such a great friend. She would come by early in the morning, get Steven up, feed him breakfast, and take him to school. Then she took care of me until I could take care of myself.

Laurie wanted to see her name written on the chalkboard at AA, which listed those sober for thirty, sixty, and ninety days. But she couldn't get past ten days sober. She learned from the AA "Big Book" that change and strength come from belief in a higher power, but this idea was difficult for Laurie; she had prayed repeatedly as a child and never gotten any help.

Laurie was angry at God, and now she was supposed to turn to Him? She'd tried to lead more of a Christian life in college, but she still had to deal with her childhood baggage. Though scared and confused, Laurie knew she couldn't live sober without divine help.

So, she prayed for an understanding, forgiving God— not the vengeful one her parents had taught her about. She needed help to quit drinking and swore to turn her life over to God. Laurie sought out an AA sponsor and read the entire Big Book, realizing that she was powerless against alcohol and that she would have to confront her fears and her past in order to live a functional life.

Laurie followed the AA program, through which her sponsor introduced a loving God, not a punisher. Laurie relapsed numerous times but started over each time.

Though Laurie loved Washington, she needed to get away. Without a job, home, or plan of any kind, she moved to south Texas with seven-year-old Steven, two cats, and a guinea pig. All Laurie had there were a few friends willing to lend a hand. "I took a risk, trusting only in God," she says.

Laurie has been in recovery for sixteen years, including ten years of continuous sobriety from alcohol and drugs. Her sobriety date is July 3, 2006. "Alcoholics Anonymous is home," she says. "It's a place where I belong. It's the fellowship that I can connect with, because only they understand me."

Laurie, now forty-seven, has her eyes on the fourteen-years-sober mark in 2020. At that point, her years of sobriety will equal her years of using.

In *Finding My Own Voice: A Story of Abuse, Addiction, and Freedom,* Laurie points out that she is much more than her alcoholism. She is a wife, mother, teacher, and student.

Eleven years ago, Laurie was working part-time at a restaurant while studying for a teaching certificate. That's when she met her husband, John, also a teacher. She knows John loves her unconditionally.

John helped Laurie raise Steven, and the couple has two more children together. Matthew and Annemarie have never seen their mom smoke, drink, or do drugs. Laurie proudly reports that Steven graduated high school with honors and joined the Air Force. He married his high school sweetheart and has a baby girl.

"He's been my rock," she says. Twenty-three years old, Steven doesn't drink or use drugs. "All he's ever wanted, since he was ten, was to get married and have kids," Laurie says.

Laurie's own education experience has been…lengthy. She loves to learn and worked hard to get through school. Laurie attended nine colleges in all.

She began college at eighteen and graduated with a Bachelor of Science degree in criminal justice at twenty-six. She then earned a master's degree in public affairs at thirty-one. Laurie went back to school to get a teaching certificate at the age of thirty-five. Later, with her husband's support, she returned to school again and earned a doctorate in education policy, leadership, and research at the age of forty-five.

Laurie loves her job teaching history and government at a middle school in Portland, Texas. A thousand students, perhaps fifteen hundred, have passed through her classroom doors. She says she is able to connect with some students in ways that others might not.

Occasionally, she will sense that a student needs extra attention. Those who do open up to her feel they can relate to someone who has been through trying times herself, whether it's physical abuse, drugs, alcohol, or all three. "On rare occasions," Laurie says, "I have shared my story with a few students, and we cried together."

She feels fortunate to be a teacher and is always glad to help struggling students. Laurie understands that learning can be especially difficult when life is a mess at home. She encourages those with bad home lives to find their own family, people who care for them and are a joy to be around.

Laurie now knows what happened to her as a child was not her fault. God didn't hate her, but rather God rescued her. "For me, acceptance was the key," she says. Real change was possible only when Laurie admitted she was an alcoholic like her father, when she fully surrendered.

Laurie has a lot of regrets. She knows she made many poor decisions and hurt people. She sometimes wishes she could start over, but she would choose the same path again, because it brought her to God.

Since getting sober, Laurie has reconnected with her mom. Though she doesn't agree with the things her mother did, Laurie realizes her mom did the best she could. Laurie was able to forgive her mother and hasn't forgotten she was there when Laurie most needed her, helping to raise Steven as a baby and toddler, which enabled Laurie to get a college degree while working.

Laurie decided to write her book after several women in her small community were killed over a period of a few years as a direct result of abuse. Too many of the wounded remain silent, Laurie says, so she came out to be a voice for victims. Accounts from survivors are what make the difference in breaking the cycle of abuse and addiction, she says.

Laurie's dad got into treatment in Washington after Laurie tried to shoot him, but there were other victims. Today he is serving life in prison for sex crimes, clinging to life after a major stroke.

Laurie no longer hates her father but chooses not to have any contact with him. She writes:

> Remember: Forgiveness isn't saying that I don't remember. It just means that I no longer hold onto it. It's a choice. I choose not to waste my energy on hate and ugliness, but to spend it on what makes me happy.

Most importantly, Laurie has forgiven herself. In her book, she explains that difficult process:

> When I sobered up, it literally hurt to look in the mirror. Therefore, I taped up sheets of construction

paper to the bathroom mirrors and took down mirrors on the walls in my house, because I hated what stared back at me.

When the paper fell off my mirrors, I had to look at myself and say out loud to my reflection that *I forgive you.* I said it every day for about a year, reminding myself that I was no longer physiologically and emotionally sick, that it was okay to let go and move on with my life. Somehow deep inside myself, I felt that I didn't deserve to be forgiven. I felt dirty for a long time, worried that I was never going to be clean and worthy for someone to love. If I was ever going to have a normal, functioning relationship with a man, I had to love and forgive myself. If I didn't, then I would never break free of the bondage of self.

As long as she stays sober, Laurie realizes she has a chance at the life she has always wanted. She has even been asked to join her community's coalition to fight against family violence. "So many great things are emerging," she says, beaming. "There are so many needs, and I hope that my story will either heal or wake people up."

Writing her story has been a work in progress for fifteen years. Laurie wrote a bit at a time. Putting her experiences on paper helped her recover from her wounds. She cried over every page and dedicated the book to God, to her husband and children, and to victims of child abuse and addiction.

Dr. Laurie Turner didn't have positive parental influence as a child. Yet she pulled herself out of an incredibly dark situation to be a guiding light for others.

Laurie puts it best:

> Statistics suggest that I should not be able to hold onto a career, live in a nice home, be married for the last ten years, and have normal, functioning children while achieving a doctorate, and most importantly, becoming a productive member of society. People like me are called survivors and those who don't survive are either dead, mentally ill, or addicts. I am not saying that I am perfect—hell no. I am severely dysfunctional…but somehow through it all, I have managed to hold onto life. I never gave up, I remained teachable, and God has always provided individuals to come into my life when I needed them most. For that I am truly thankful.
>
> All I ever wanted were acceptance and love. It is quite simple: I drank and used because I wanted love. That's all anybody wants.

........................................................................

If you would like to make a donation in honor of Dr. Laurie Turner, please do so at the Palmer Drug Abuse Program (PDAP), in Corpus Christi, Texas, which focuses on young people and addiction (pdapcc.org).

# Nick

No one envisioned Nicholas James Vujicic would lead a wonderful and inspiring life—especially not him. Born with no arms and no legs, Nick seemed doomed to a sad existence marked by disability and loneliness.

Instead, Nick is a world-renowned speaker and author, whose story has inspired millions of people across the globe. As Nick says:

> The fact is that as mere mortals, you and I have limited vision. We can't possibly see what lies ahead…My encouragement to you is that what lies ahead may be far better than anything you ever thought possible.

Nick came into the world December 4, 1982, in Melbourne, Australia. His parents, Dushka and Boris Vujicic (pronounced VOO-yee-cheech), are devout Christians from Serbia (in the former Yugoslavia), whose families had immigrated to Australia to escape Communist oppression. Dushka, twenty-five when Nick was born, had been a midwife and pediatric nurse, and although her pregnancy had progressed smoothly and three ultrasounds showed no abnormalities, her intuition told her something wasn't right.

After she delivered Nick, Dushka wasn't able to see her son at first, but she could tell by the way the hospital staff acted that something was seriously wrong. The doctor told Dushka and Boris their newborn had tetra-amelia syndrome, also known as phocomelia, which means "having no arms or legs." There is no known medical reason for this condition.

Unsure what to do, the shocked parents considered putting Nick up for adoption, but their strong faith won out. They believed a higher plan was in play, so they would do their best, trusting God for the rest.

Nick had been born with a small left foot, which had two toes fused together. (He has an even smaller right foot, as well.) His doctors performed an operation to separate Nick's toes, which later allowed him to use his toes like fingers, enabling him to hold a pen and perform other tasks such as operating an electric wheelchair, using a computer, and operating a cell phone. The Lions Club in the community raised more than $200,000 to cover the family's medical bills and provide a wheelchair for Nick.

Nick had a surprisingly normal childhood. He was resourceful and active. Nick quickly learned to use his forehead against a stable surface to raise himself up. His parents repeatedly reminded him he was God's creation and could do nearly anything he set his mind to, despite his physical limitations.

He loved soccer, playing with marbles, skateboarding, and fishing with his dad. Nick also enjoyed tormenting his younger siblings, Aaron and Michelle. Life was filled with faith, fun, and laughter.

But sometimes other kids would keep their distance. Nick was uncomfortable, but he approached them at his parents' behest; they said others would warm up to Nick once they got to know him.

He recalls on his website, lifewithoutlimbs.org:

> I used to get teased a lot and would come home crying. But day by day my parents would tell me to just smile back at people, start talking and playing as much as I can with them so they would know I'm just like them. It started to make a difference.

Yet Nick grew increasingly insecure. He was bullied and called "freak" and "alien," hurtful names to an already sensitive boy. He poked fun at himself to get by, but sometimes he hid in empty classrooms or in the bushes to avoid humiliation.

At the age of ten, Nick began refusing to go to school, tired of the ribbing he endured. Despite the happy and brave exterior he showed publicly, he was angry at God. He felt unheard and often cried in bed at night asking God to give him arms and legs. The future looked hopeless; Nick figured he'd never have a decent job or a girlfriend, not to mention a wife and kids. He felt alone and without purpose, nothing more than a burden to others.

One evening while his mom cooked dinner, Nick thought about throwing himself off the kitchen counter. He reasoned he might be able to break his neck and end his misery. But Nick thought better of it, because he'd have to explain himself to his family if he didn't succeed.

A few days later, Nick devised a new plan. After school one day, he asked his mom to put him in the bathtub to soak. Floating on his back, Nick rolled over, face down. After some time, he turned back over, gasping for air. His daily pain was too much to handle, so Nick went back under water again. When he did, an image of his parents and younger brother crying over his grave flashed in his head. They felt responsible for Nick's death, which he couldn't bear. He surfaced for air once again.

That night, Nick told seven-year-old Aaron he would kill himself at the age of twenty-one. Nick reasoned he could get through high school and college, but after that there would be nothing for him to live for. He then fell asleep, only to be awakened by his father.

Nick's dad, an accountant and lay pastor, sat on his bed, asking him what this talk of suicide was about. His father promised Nick that he and Dushka would always be there for their son no matter what, and that good things were in store for Nick. His dad's reassurances picked up his spirits. Nick still has occasional down days even now, but he never considered suicide again after that day.

Often it is darkest right before dawn.

Nick got through high school and went to college at Griffith University in Logan, Queensland. He earned a Bachelor of Commerce degree at the age of twenty-one, double majoring in accounting and financial planning. He assumed he'd follow in his father's footsteps to become an accountant, dreaming of starting his own business.

But before Nick finished college, an unexpected experience changed the course of his life. Due to his unique condition, good sense of humor, and outgoing personality, church and student groups asked Nick to do speaking engagements. He began sharing his story about the struggles he'd faced—cautiously at first—and was surprised to find people were touched emotionally. More invitations to talk to youth groups and churches followed.

A turning point occurred when Nick shared his testimony at a high school in Australia. About three hundred people listened to Nick, including a girl who sobbed uncontrollably when she met him. She hugged Nick, thanking him for changing her life.

That's when Nick first realized that sharing his story could give others hope. He says:

> In that moment, when I realized that I had made a huge difference in that girl's life in a meaningful and positive way, the thrill that I felt was beyond anything I had ever experienced up to that point in my life. The joy and peace that came over me in knowing that this was my true calling was undeniable. From that day onward, my undying passion was to speak hope and love into another person's life wherever and whenever God prompted me.

He recalls another crucial moment in his life, when he heard an American motivational speaker at an assembly when he was in high school. Nick realized maybe he, too, could build a career as a public speaker. After all, traveling around the world and getting paid to give people hope seemed really cool.

Nick felt called to talk about his struggles and his faith, to provide hope to anyone who'd listen. Nick threw himself into his new passion with a fierce determination and vigor, and his life took off. The more he talked, the more his confidence grew and the more his message spread. His dedication paid off; he was soon sought out for engagements that have had him touring the world ever since.

He'd found his purpose as a speaker and evangelist:

> Recognizing your purpose means everything. I assure you that you, too, have something to contribute. You may not see it now, but you would not be on this planet if that were not true. I know for certain that God does not make mistakes, but he does make miracles. I am one. You are, too.

Nick came to believe that each of us has a gift, the pursuit of which leads to happiness. And to be truly fulfilled, one must serve others. He explains:

> Looking back at all I had to overcome at such a young age—the pain, the insecurity, the hurt, the loneliness—I don't feel sad. I feel humbled and grateful, because I overcame those challenges that make my successes all the sweeter. In the end, they

made me stronger, and, more important, they made
me better equipped to reach out to others. Without
my pain, I would never be able to help anybody else
deal with their pain. I wouldn't be able to relate so
well with other people.

In 2010, at age twenty-seven, Nick co-wrote his first book,
*Life Without Limits: Inspiration for a Ridiculously Good Life*,
to share his story with more people and to help readers
develop a deeper relationship with God. He also presides
over an international nonprofit ministry, Life Without
Limbs, founded in 2005.

His website explains:

Life Without Limbs is all about sharing this same
hope and genuine love that I have personally experienced with people all over the globe. It's been
said that doors open to a man without arms and
legs much more easily than to anyone else, and we
thank God for providing that privilege. I've been
invited into very unexpected places to share about
my faith in Jesus Christ, and literally millions have
responded.

Traveling extensively to over sixty-three countries and still counting, I have been extremely
humbled by the continuous opportunities that
the Lord has given me to share my testimony. My
greatest joy in this life is to introduce Jesus to those

I meet and tell them of His great desire to get to know them personally by allowing Him to become their Lord and Savior. That's what Life Without Limbs is all about.

Because of the ministry of Life Without Limbs, God has used me in countless schools, churches, prisons, orphanages, hospitals, stadiums and in face-to-face encounters with individuals, telling them how very precious they are to God. It is our greatest pleasure to assure people that God does have a plan for each and every life that is meaningful and purposeful, for God took my life, one that others might disregard as not having any significance, and He has filled me with His purpose and showed me His plans to use me to move hearts and lives toward Him.

After many visits to the United States (the Vujicics have a large extended family in the United States and in Australia), Nick relocated from Australia to Southern California in 2007. A friend there had offered to help him set up a ministry in the States, and Nick took the leap after a lot of prayer. Nick loves Australia, but the United States offered more exposure and opportunities. Nick's faith paid off, and Life Without Limbs soon was flooded with requests.

Nick doesn't think he would have accomplished all he has if he had been born with arms and legs. He now sees his condition as an asset that gives him instant credibility;

crowds can easily see he's had to face many challenges, which makes them more apt to listen. "I'm officially *disabled*, but I'm truly *enabled* because of my lack of limbs," he says.

Nick continues:

> What my family and I could not foresee was that my disability—my "burden"—could also be a blessing, offering me unique opportunities for reaching out to others, empathizing with them, understanding their pain, and offering them comfort. Yes, I do have distinct challenges, but I am also blessed with a loving family, with a keen enough mind, and with a deep and abiding faith. I'll be candid…neither my faith nor my sense of purpose grew strong until I went through some very scary times.

Because audience members don't always know how to approach Nick, he frequently falls back on a familiar coping mechanism from his youth: using humor as an icebreaker. For example, Nick tells kids he's just small for his age. At seventy-four pounds, he can easily fit into the overhead compartments on airplanes, which the fun-loving and mischievous Vujicic has pulled on unsuspecting passengers.

Nick is in the perfect field for his personality:

> I love people. I love meeting new people. I absolutely love talking to people. I am not a shy person. My mom often encouraged me to "just start talking" so that people could see that I was a normal guy with

only a few pieces missing. That prompting early on in my life from my mom really helped develop in me a friendly attitude, extroverted personality, and love for people.

Nick's many prayers for a life partner were answered in 2011. After sharing his goals for Life Without Limbs to a small private party in McKinney, Texas, he saw a beautiful half-Japanese, half-Mexican woman across the room. When he met Kanae (Kan-eye-AYE), the feeling was electric, love at first sight.

Nick later proposed on a yacht by asking if he could kiss Kanae's fingers. When she agreed, he used his mouth to leave a ring on her finger and asked her to be his wife. The couple married in February 2012 and now has two sons, Kiyoshi and Dejan. (Tetra-amelia is not genetic, so there was little chance they'd have a child without limbs.)

Kanae and Nick wrote a book together, *Love Without Limits: A Remarkable Story of True Love Conquering All*, released in April 2015. Kanae says Nick is "the perfect match for [her]." Their deep love is easily noticed; people sometimes approach the couple and say they believe in true love again.

"I absolutely adore her," Nick says about his wife and best friend. "She has a grace, loveliness, patience, and meekness that I respect so much. She is such a focused and gentle giver."

Nick calls himself "ridiculously happy." Now thirty-four,

he is wise enough to know that all along there was a purpose, "and it has proven to be far, far, *far* beyond anything I could have imagined."

Nick realizes that everything is much the same today as it was when he almost ended his own life. He is still without arms and legs. (Nick has tried various prosthetic and electronic arms, but nothing has been a good enough fit. He feels he can do nearly everything he needs to do without them, though he hopes with technological advancements he might be able to walk someday. He even keeps a pair of shoes in his closet just in case.)

The major difference in Nick's life now as opposed to when he attempted suicide is he focuses on his possibilities instead of his limitations. Instead of looking at his challenges as merely a hindrance, he sees them as a blessing. When Nick turned his "weakness" into a strength, his life significantly improved:

> It's important to recognize your own value. Know that you also have something to contribute. If you feel frustrated right now, that's okay. Your sense of frustration means you want more for your life than you have right now. That's all good. Often it's the challenges in life that show us who we are truly meant to be.

Many YouTube videos show Nick playing soccer, jumping off a diving board, tandem skydiving, flipping open his Bible using his toes ("fingers"), and giving his sons a ride in a stroller attached to his electric wheelchair. His videos have been watched more than one hundred million times.

Talk show legend Oprah Winfrey had Nick on one of her shows, talking about the "excruciating" path that led him to success. Nick, originally sitting with the audience in the crowd, hopped up the steps and then walked across the stage to the amazement and cheers of the audience.

Nick has told his story to 4.5 million people all over the world. He has filled stadiums. He has authored several books, including *Unstoppable: The Incredible Power of Faith in Action*, illustrating how people can respond to adversity such as addiction, disability, and career and relationship challenges; *Stand Strong: You Can Overcome Bullying (and Other Stuff That Keeps You Down)*; and the aforementioned *Love Without Limits: A Remarkable Story of True Love Conquering All*, co-written with Kanae.

Nick also has released inspirational DVDs in addition to the YouTube videos, using as many platforms as he can to spread his message. He even added acting to his resume, starring in a short film, *The Butterfly Circus*, which won the $100,000 grand prize at the Doorpost Film Project for film-makers of hopeful films.

Nick points out he's not a superhero. He is an authentic guy with struggles of his own. But he is armed with a strong faith and a burning desire to inspire others to never give up:

> Your circumstances may be difficult. You may have
> challenges with your health, your finances, or your

relationships. But with a sense of purpose, faith in your future, and determination to never give up, you can overcome any obstacle.

His hobbies include painting, swimming, and golf: "I hold a golf club between my shoulder and chin. It took lots of practice, but I'm pretty comfortable doing it now." Nick's favorite way to relax is fishing, which he accomplishes by anchoring the fishing rod between his chin and shoulder, while holding the line in his teeth until releasing at the right time to cast the line.

Though he can do pretty much anything he needs to do independently, he employs caregivers working on rotating shifts to help, especially getting him ready when traveling. The caregivers save him time that he can devote to other things—and Nick is endlessly busy.

Life Without Limbs supports more than ten charities, including sponsoring missionaries and partnering with the Joni and Friends disability ministry to donate refurbished wheelchairs. He has visited some of the darkest corners of the world, but he still sees joy and brings hope everywhere he goes. He references Mother Teresa's belief and example that even a small kindness can produce a chain reaction of good in the world.

That's why Nick suggests that his audience members stop focusing so much on themselves and their own trying circumstances. Instead of looking for pity, seek someone you can help, he tells them. After all, "Most of the hardships we face provide us with opportunities to discover who we are meant to be and what we can share of our gifts to benefit others."

He recommends people step out of their comfort zone in order to thrive and grow.

"Keep moving ahead, because action creates momentum, which in turn creates unanticipated opportunities," Nick says. "The place between your comfort zone and your dream is where life takes place."

..................................................................

If you would like to learn more about Nick Vujicic, or make a donation in his honor, you can do so at lifewithoutlimbs. org.

# Acknowledgments

I owe a debt of gratitude to everyone discussed in this book for their willingness to be a part of this project; I really appreciate your time and cooperation. Thank you for the wonderful work you do to make this world a better place. Much appreciation also to Abby Richter at John O'Leary Inspires, Bev Garcia at Life Without Limbs, and Molly Wade at Not Impossible for all of your help.

To all of my family and friends, especially my parents, Pat and Jolinda Maginn, thank you for your continued support, interest, and encouragement.

Thank you to Lori Highlander for giving me the opportunity with *(Extra)Ordinary: Inspirational Stories of Everyday People* and for inviting me back again for this book. You have a wonderful team at KiCam Projects, and I am grateful to everyone who had a hand in turning my manuscript into this book.

Special thanks to KiCam's Jennifer Scroggins—the Wizard of Oz behind the scenes—for your fantastic assistance in vastly improving my book. Working with you is a pleasure and I appreciate your invaluable feedback. I am fortunate that you are so good at your job.

Lastly, thank you, dear reader, for reading my book. If you enjoyed this book, I would greatly appreciate a review on Amazon.com. Thank you for your support.

Until next time, all the best…
Keith Maginn